131 AL

Fiat

Books in the Rally Giants Series

written by Graham Robson and published by Veloce Publishing

Ford Escort Mk1

Lancia Stratos

Subaru Impreza

Austin Healey 100-6 & 3000

Peugeot 205 T16

Ford Escort RS1800

Audi Quattro

Ford Escort RS Cosworth & World Rally Car

Fiat 131 Abarth

Mini Cooper/Mini Cooper S

Toyota Celica GT-Four

Saab 96 & V4

Lancia Delta 4WD/Integrale

www.veloce.co.uk

First published in October 2008 by Veloce Publishing Limited, Veloce House, Parkway Farm Business Park, Middle Farm Way, Poundbury, Dorchester DT1 3AR, England. Fax 01305 250479 / e-mail info@veloce.co.uk / web www.veloce.co.uk or www.velocebooks.com. Reprinted March 2017.

ISBN: 978-1-787111-11-0 UPC: 6-36847-01111-6

Readers with ideas for automotive books, or books on other transport or related hobby subjects, are invited to write to the editorial director of Veloce Publishing at the above address. British Library Cataloguing in Publication Data - A catalogue record for this book is available from the British Library. Typesetting, design and page make-up all by Veloce Publishing Ltd on Apple Mac. Printed and bound by CPI Group (UK) Ltd, Croydon, CR0 4YY.

RALLY GIANTS

131 Abarth

Fiat

Graham Robson

Contents

Foreword

What is a rally? Today's events, for sure, are completely different from those of a hundred or even fifty years ago. What was once a test of reliability is now a test of speed and strength. What was once a long-distance trial is now a series of short-distance races.

In the beginning, rallying was all about using standard cars in long-distance road events, but by the 1950s the events were toughening up. Routes became rougher, target speeds were raised, point-to-point speed tests on special stages were introduced, and high-performance machines were needed to ensure victory.

Starting in the late 1950s, too, teams began developing extra-special versions of standard cars, these were built

in small numbers, and were meant only to go rallying or motor racing. These 'homologation specials' now dominate the sport. The first of these, unquestionably, was the Austin-Healey 3000, and the latest is any one of the ten-off World Rally Cars which we see on our TV screens or on the special stages of the world.

Although rally regulations changed persistently over the years, the two most important events were four-wheel drive being authorised from 1980, and the 'World Rally Car' formula (which required only 20 identical cars to be produced to gain homologation) being adopted in 1997. At all times, however, successful rally cars have needed to blend high performance with strength and reliability. Unlike

Grand Prix cars, they have needed to be built so that major repairs could be carried out at the side of the road, in the dark, sometimes in freezing cold, and sometimes in blazing temperatures.

Over the years, some cars became dominant, only to be eclipsed when new and more advanced rivals appeared. New cars appeared almost every year, but dramatically better machines appeared less often. From time to time rally enthusiasts would be astonished by a new model, and it was on occasions like that when a new rallying landmark was set.

So, which were the most important new cars to appear in the last half century? What is it that made them special at the time? In some cases it was perfectly obvious – Lancia's Stratos was the first-ever purpose-built rally car, the Audi Quattro was the first rally-winning four-wheel drive car, and the Toyota Celica GT4 was the first rally-winning four-wheel drive Group A car to come from Japan.

But what about Ford's amazing Escort? Or the tiny but effective Mini-Cooper S? Or the Fiat 131 Abarth covered in this book? Or the Lancia Delta Integrale? Or, of course, the Subaru Impreza? All of them had something unique to offer at the time, in comparison with their competitors. Because they offered something different, and raised rallying's standards even further, they were true Rally Giants.

To a rallying petrol-head like me, it would have been easy to choose twenty, thirty or even more rally cars that have made a difference to the sport. However, I have had to be brutal and cull my list to the very minimum. Listed here, in chronological order, are the 'Giant' cars I have picked out, to tell the on-going story of world-class rallying in the last fifty years:

Car	Period used as a works car
Austin-Healey 100-Six and 3000	1959-1965
Saab 96 and V4	1960-1976
Mini-Cooper/Cooper S	1962-1970
Ford Escort Mk I	1968-1975
Lancia Stratos	1974-1981
Ford Escort (Mk II) RS1800	1975-1981
Fiat 131 Abarth	1976-1981
Audi Quattro and S1	1981-1986
Peugeot 205T16	1984-1986
Lancia Delta 4x4/Integrale	1987-1993
Toyota Celica GT4	1988-1995
Ford Escort RS Cosworth/WRC	1993-1998
Subaru Impreza Turbo/WRC	1993-2006

There is so much to know, to tell, and to enjoy about these cars that I plan to devote a compact book to each one. And to make sure that one can be compared with another, I intend to keep the same format for each volume.

Graham Robson

6

Visit Veloce on the web – www.veloce.co.uk
Details of all books in print • Special offers • New book news • Gift vouchers

Introduction & acknowledgements

In spite of several in-built drawbacks to its basic design – the engine was never powerful enough, and parts of the transmission were often likely to break on arduous rallies – between 1976 and 1981 the Fiat 131 Abarth was a hugely successful car. As with its big rival the Ford Escort RS1800, works 131 Abarths were ultra-competitive until the Audi Quattro arrived – after which they swiftly became obsolete.

I have always admired the Fiat 131 Abarth – and respected the Italian team which developed and campaigned the car. How many other organisations, after all, would have relished being dragged away from the world-class Lancia Stratos, being told to abandon that mid-engined supercar to its fate, and being directed to produce another world-beating rally car, this time around a family saloon?

Stated simply, and quite baldly, in 1975 Fiat's publicists decided that they wanted to see a recognisable Fiat-based saloon car winning rallies, rather than a space-age two-seater which might have carried almost any badge on its nose. Having nominated Abarth (the tuning business which it owned) to do the engineering job, Fiat also obliged that company to abandon work that had been started on a 2-litre-engined Fiat X1/9 rally car project.

Because Fiat wanted a new-generation works rally car to have strong links with the Fiat family cars that sold in hundreds of thousands every year, the only 'donor' car which then made sense was the newly-launched 131. Although tightly constrained as to what it could change and what had to be left alone, Abarth (not Fiat) went ahead and transformed this into a truly formidable rally car.

When I was formulating my original list of Rally Giants, I included the 131 Abarth for two very important reasons – it laid the foundation for Fiat to win the World Rally Championship for Makes three times (in 1977, 1978 and 1980), and it took the concept of 'building a better Escort' to a new level of technical excellence.

In the case of the Fiat, however, I should emphasise that it was only the Abarth-prepared works cars (and there were fifty of them over the years) which could regularly win at top level. Very few of the balance of the 'homologation build' (which means another 350 cars, as will be explained in the text) were ever prepared to full works/Abarth levels. Cars which won European or prestigious National Championship events (those held in France, Germany and Italy being perfect examples) had invariably been prepared, or re-prepared from older works cars by Abarth, before being sold on. (Competitive privately-owned Escorts, however, were built in their hundreds, and were still winning at international level in 1983 and 1984.)

The 131 Abarth programme was successful in almost every way. Although company politics got in the way of the development of a truly Escort-competitive engine (the Fiat unit had far too long a stroke, which top management would never agree to alter), every other aspect of the car was designed for one job and one job alone – to make the works rally car competitive, and capable of refinement for all sorts of events.

Compared with the Escort RS1800 – and, make no mistake, Fiat incessantly measured the 131's performance against that of the British car – the 131 Abarth had a more advanced chassis, complete with independent rear suspension which was adjustable in so many ways. This meant that it could, and often did, make up for a lack of straight-line performance with handling and traction which was measurably superior to those of its rivals. Additionally, the works team was always run with remarkable flair, consistency, guile, competence and – how the rivals moaned about this – a very generous budget. Fiat wanted to see World Championships won, and Abarth duly delivered. All this, matched by the hiring of superlative drivers – not least Markku Alan and Walter Röhrl – made the 131 Abarth team an object lesson of how to go rallying.

When the time came for the 131 Abarth to be replaced, a superlative new machine would be needed – which is where, and why, the Lancia Rally 037 was born. But that, as they say, is an entirely different story ....

Acknowledgements

As ever, I want to thank the many people who helped me assemble all the facts and figures which complete this book. Although I was always close to the rally scene when the 131 Abarth was in its prime, considerable research was necessary before these words could be written, and the pages illustrated.

I want to start by admitting that much of the book would have needed further editing if Sergio Limone, that wonderfully helpful ex-Abarth engineer, had not helped me so much. Sergio, who worked on the 131 Abarth as a young man, and would later lead the design team which produced the Lancia Rally 037 and Delta Integrale rally cars, was a mine of information, and a visit to see him in Turin was a real privilege.

British historic rallying enthusiast, Mick Wood, who probably knows as much about these cars as any other owner, has kept an ex-works car and loves everything to do with them. Not only did Mick put me in touch with Sergio Limone, but he was kind enough to let me study the homologation papers and much more of the written material which Abarth published about these cars.

Cesare Fiorio, the distinguished motorsport boss at Lancia and the Fiat-Abarth team has, over the years, always been ready to provide insight, facts and opinion about the career of this and other related models.

Naturally, when it came to the search for images, and for facts and figures about World Rallies, I needed to rely on the expertise and knowledge of Martin Holmes. As I have stated on several previous occasions, Martin's *World Rallying* annuals are a constant source of inspiration, and his personal pictorial archive is a gold mine too. I have come to rely on Martin as an absolute authority, to be cherished at all times.

To all of them, and other unsung heroes whom I also consulted, I hope I have been able to assemble the authentic story of Fiat's greatest-ever rally car.

Visit Veloce on the web – www.veloce.co.uk
Details of all books in print • Special offers • New book news • Gift vouchers

8

The car and the team

Inspiration

The car which became Fiat's most successful rally vehicle was Abarth's pragmatic and successful response to a request from Fiat's marketing department. It wanted to see something that looked like a mass-market family car winning on the special stages of the world. Success with the exotic 124 Abarth Rallye was one thing, and with the Lancia Stratos (nearly a 'blood relation,' since Fiat owned Lancia) another, but these were sports cars after all. And at the time, a proposed competition car replacement from Abarth – a 2-litre 124 Abarth-engined development of the mid-engined Fiat X1/9 – was already evolving on the same lines.

The X1/9 was chosen instead of the new Lancia Beta Monte Carlo (also known internally as the X1/20), not only because it was smaller and lighter than the Stratos, and therefore also the Beta Monte Carlo, but because it was a Fiat-badged, as opposed to a Lancia-badged, car. Work progressed so fast that Abarth had already built four competition car prototypes, and a proposed road car/homologation version, before it was told to stop work immediately.

By 1975, company sentiment was swinging decisively behind the 'family car which wins' concept, as Fiat realised just how much it had done for Ford's Escort. In April of that year, therefore, the big decision was made to cancel the X1/9 project, just as its limited production run was about to begin, and to start afresh on the newly-launched 131 model. Progress, thereafter, was swift, for the very first (Group 5-specification) prototype competed in an event in November 1975, and homologation (on rather

The first specially-engineered Fiat for rally use was the 124 Abarth Rallye which was announced in 1972. In general layout but not in detail the 131 Abarth would evolve from this.

9

Fiat – newcomers at World level

It's worth remembering that when Fiat announced the 131 Abarth in 1976, it was still a relative newcomer to modern world-class rallying. Until 1970, the company had been more concerned with supporting Abarth in motor racing than in rallying, and the very first works cars had been built in-house within the Fiat workshops, supported by the Assistenza Tecnica department. The team, though, soon

flimsy evidence concerning the production figures already achieved) followed in April 1976.

What came after, in so many ways, was a rewriting of the Ford Escort story. With similar influences, timetables and production claims to those that had been made in 1967 and 1968, and starting with a very mundane and unpromising family saloon, Abarth, on Fiat's behalf, achieved the same sort of miracles.

Compared with the standard 124 Spider road car, the 124 Abarth Rallye was lighter, more powerful (it had a 16-valve engine for 1975), and had independent rear suspension.

settled at the Abarth premises at Corso Marche in Turin. The buildings themselves were long established and by no means high-tech – as one wise old sage once commented: "No, they were certainly not up to McLaren levels of cleanliness ...". Originally, Fiat used big and uncompetitive 125 saloons, whose only merit was a fine Lampredi-designed 1.6-litre 8-valve twin-cam engine (Håkan Lindberg of Sweden was the first works driver), but these cars were soon supplanted by 124 Sport Spiders. At least they looked the part, being two-seaters, and obviously more sporting.

Amazingly, a Spider then won the rough and tough Acropolis Rally in 1972, which proved that the structures were already very strong, but it was not until the 1.8-litre

124 Abarth Rallye (a two-seater sports car with independent rear suspension, much lightened, which always ran with a permanent hardtop in place) took over, in 1973, that Fiat became truly competitive in many of the world's top events.

It was the 124 Abarth Rallye and its 16-valve evolution, of course, which provided most of the inspiration for the running gear of the 131 Abarth, though there was considerable change in almost every detail. The 124 Abarth Rallye recorded outright wins in 1973 (Poland), 1974 (Portugal) and 1975 (Portugal/TAP). By then it had been re-homologated, with a new-type 16-valve twin-cam cylinder head in an engine which produced up to 200bhp,

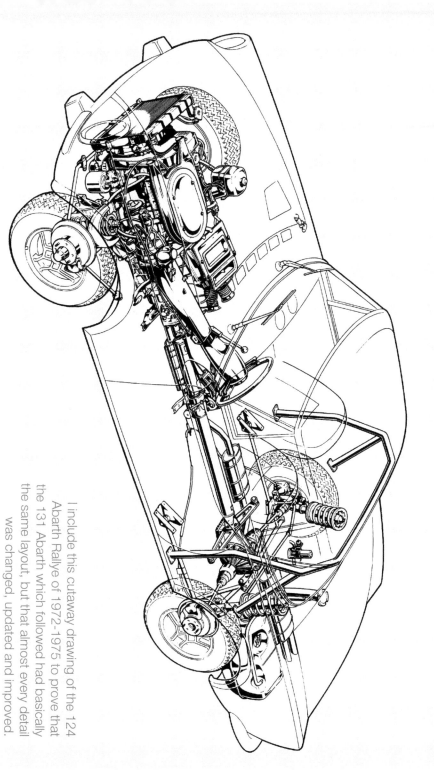

I include this cutaway drawing of the 124 Abarth Rallye of 1972-1975 to prove that the 131 Abarth which followed had basically the same layout, but that almost every detail was changed, updated and improved.

Although the 124 Abarth Rallye was always sturdy, it was not powerful enough – and the 131 Abarth project would have to deal with that deficiency. This was Rauno Aaltonen and Robin Turvey on their way to second place in the Acropolis Rally of 1973.

and it was from that car that much of the general layout of the 131 model developed. However, the 124 was still neither as fast, nor as sophisticated, as some its front-line opposition, and something much better would be needed to match up to the new Lancia Stratos, and the ever-versatile Ford Escort, in the years to come.

Fiat showed no lack of commitment with the 124 Abarth Rallye, but it needed a more advanced car for the late 1970s. This was Hannu Mikkola and Jean Todt in the Arctic Rally of 1975.

Maturity but not quite enough speed on the Monte Carlo Rally of 1975. The works 124 Abarth Rallyes took second, third and fourth places, behind Sandro Munari's winning Lancia Stratos. Markku Alén, driving this car, took third place.

The 124 Abarth Rallye was familiar and successful by 1975. Here was the Verini/Rosetti works car in the 1975 RAC Rally, on its way to eighth place.

The 131 Abarth's importance in rallying

For Fiat, of course, success in World Rallying was vital, as the newly-launched 131 family car marketing support at all levels. Up until then, Fiat's works cars had not only been sports cars (which did not appeal to as a wide an audience as the saloons), but they were neither pretty, nor impressive – nor truly competitive.

By 1975, Fiat had already been in the sport for five years. It had seen just how glamorous it was for cars like the in-house rival, Lancia, to be winning, and it had also seen how effective the successful Ford Escort had been in boosting the image of an otherwise rather mundane range of small family cars. It realised, full-well, that although the rally-winning Fords – complete with their 16-valve 2-litre engines, special transmissions and special suspensions – bore no mechanical

This was why the world's rallying public loved the Stratos – it always looked and sounded spectacular. Raffaele Pinto on his way to fourth place in Portugal in 1976. The 131 Abarth was just ready for homologation.

Ford's ubiquitous Escort RS1800 was the 131 Abarth's principal rival during the 1976–1981 period, and always had a much more powerful 2-litre engine. This was Hannu Mikkola on his way to winning the 1978 RAC Rally.

relation to the mass-market show-room Escorts, the buying public neither knew, nor cared, about that.

The true importance of the 131 Abarth project, therefore, was not that Fiat had finally decided to let its subsidiary, Abarth, have its head to design the best possible car, but that if successful, it was going to change the face of World Rallying in many events. Although there were

practical and financial limits to the re-engineering which Abarth was allowed to carry out on the 131, like the Lancia Stratos which was approaching maturity with up to 500 cars completed (partly by Bertone, partly by Lancia itself), this was as near to a 'hang the expense' project as made no difference.

In sporting terms, though, the 131 Abarth was important

because it would add to the glamour of the sport at the very highest level. In 1974 and 1975, when the concept of a radically new Fiat rally car began to emerge, World Rallying was dominated by just four marques – Lancia with the Stratos, Ford with the Escort RS1600/RS1800 models, Fiat itself, and, to a lesser extent, Alpine-Renault, whose A110s were now over the hill. Until and unless Toyota, with a European base and a Swedish manager, could produce a competitive car, that was about the height of it.

As far as Fiat was concerned, this was exactly the right time to invest heavily in a new car, especially if it could come to an agreement with Lancia not to compete head-on, too often or too obviously. By using its respected sub-contractors at Bertone, who had done such a great job in producing 500 monocoque structures for the Lancia Stratos, and at Abarth, where much of the engineering and development would take place, Fiat could plan logically for producing the 400 cars which Group 4 regulations then demanded.

In broader worldwide rallying terms, the evolution of the new Fiat was obviously attractive to several loyal but privately-financed teams which had rather quailed at the thought of rallying Ferrari-engined Lancia Stratos cars. It meant that, in broad terms, there could be a more interesting and competitive selection of rally cars on the special stages of Europe, and maybe even the world, in the late 1970s. And, most of all, Fiat hoped that it could look forward to rallying success with a mainstream brand.

Facing up to rival cars

Fiat was already an experienced entrant in World Championship rallies when it came to develop the 131 Abarth. Having entered the sport with a long-term commitment to success, and with the technical backing of top management, it had already transformed the 124 Spider into the very effective 124 Abarth Rallye. What followed would be a logical step forward – and the company already knew what all its rivals were planning.

Due to the fact that the 131 Abarth was not really an all-new model, but, mechanically at least, a major evolution of the running gear of the existing 124 Abarth Rallye, Fiat

immediately realised what improvements ought to be made. Experience in the field, in particular, had shown it where the 124 needed to be improved, and what might be achieved with new engineering and enterprising homologation.

There were two major objectives: one was to enlarge the engine to make it more powerful, more torquey, and more easily fettled and rebuilt between (and even on!) events; the other was to make the transmission more robust. The Lancia Stratos, an 'in-house' competitor, the Porsche 911 and, of course, Ford's Escort RS1800 all had more power and winning track records. Unlike the Lancia and the Porsche, but not (significantly, as we would soon find out) the Ford Escort, its traction would be suspect. As it was a normal, mid-size family saloon, the engine was located upfront, and would stay that way. For rallying, therefore, the 131 lacked the very desirable feature of an engine-over-the-driving-wheels layout, and nothing could be done to deal with that.

In 1975 and 1976, when the 131 Abarth was being engineered and made ready for production, these were its principal competitors:

Ford Escort RS1800 – front-engine/rear-drive. Already a winner at World level, this was a car that had evolved from Mk I types (the Twin-Cam and the RS1600). Ideally sized – with 250bhp/2-litres and a five-speed transmission – after eight years of development it was as rugged and as versatile as Ford Motorsport could possibly make it. By this time, though, there was little more to be done to improve the cars, which were already close to their performance peak.

Where traction was already available, it was one of the fastest rally cars in the world, but on ice, snow and loose-surface going, it was a car which always struggled to find grip. Ford, with no suitable choice in the range, always tried to idealise these cars, and in Europe at least they were formidable competitors with a great track record.

Ford also had a big motorsport marketing advantage. Because it was its policy to make all the special parts available in numbers, private owners could, and did, build up 'works-replicas.' Large numbers of such cars, therefore,

Fiat also owned Lancia, but until 1977 the two brands were always rivals. Earlier in the 1970s, Lancia had designed the mid-engined Stratos, which was a world-beater until Fiat decided that it should be 'retired' from competition. This was Sandro Munari on his way to victory in the 1977 Monte Carlo Rally – his third Monte victory in three years. The 131 Abarth could not match the pace of this machine.

were used on every continent. They won hundreds, if not thousands, of international events.

It is now known that Fiat was so concerned with the reputation of these cars that before finalising the design of the 131 Abarth, the company made arrangements to secretly hire an RS1800 (from David Sutton), to test and analyse

it. They found that although the engine was astonishingly powerful, the handling and traction were constrained by the live axle layout.

Lancia Stratos – mid-engine/rear-drive. In the mid-1970s, this was the ultimate weapon, the world's first purpose-designed rally car. Small, very fast (it had a Ferrari Dino 2.4-litre V6 engine, often in 290bhp/24-valve form), and designed to be ideal for rough-road and tarmac rallying, it was also backed by a stupendously high-budget operation from Fiat-Lancia. It was only bad luck, it seemed, which stopped a works Stratos from winning every time it started a World Rally. Ford, and the Escort Mk II, had no real counter to this – except for reliability. Fiat-Lancia politics eventually saw the Stratos sidelined, in favour of the Fiat 131 Abarth. Ford and other rivals were relieved about that!

Porsche 911 – rear-engine/rear-drive. First used (as a 2-litre) in 1965, but by 1974 with a 250bhp/2.7-litre engine. Superb traction and, in the right hands, still capable of winning on any surface. Although it had won three Monte Carlo rallies, and many other European events, the 911 was never campaigned hard and consistently by the Porsche factory, which preferred to go motor racing instead. This delighted Fiat, especially as a 3-litre version of the 911 would

The Lancia Stratos was always competitive but sometimes fragile. This was Sandro Munari in San Remo in 1977, when the transmission broke. Victory, instead, would go to Andruet's works 131 Abarth.

In addition to those above, although it did not know it in 1976, Fiat would eventually be facing serious competition from the following cars:

Saab 99 Turbo – front-engine/front-drive. Totally different from the Saab V4, these bigger/heavier cars had turbocharged versions of the latest 2-litre engines, with 250-270bhp in works form, and would first be seen in late 1978. Solid, near unbreakable on rough events, and nimble on snow and ice, they were excellent cars for Scandinavian conditions. Not ideal for tarmac use – they were too heavy – and not backed by a big-enough programme budget, they were eventually withdrawn when found to be uncompetitive against Ford and Fiat.

Talbot Sunbeam-Lotus – front-engine/rear-drive. Like the Vauxhall Chevette HS (see below), this was another manufacturer's idea of what a 'better Escort' might be like, a Group 4 car with a 240bhp 2.2-litre four-cylinder engine

soon appear, along with a turbocharged derivative which ought to have been unbeatable. So much potential was still locked away inside the 911 that it was competitive until the mid-1980s, years after the 131 Abarth had been retired.

Saab V4 – front-engine/front-drive. First used in 1968, though the structure, basic layout, and rallying experience of the works team all dated from 1960. With an homologated 1.8-litre (Ford Germany) V4 engine from 1971, up to 165bhp, and with great drivers like Stig Blomqvist, this excellent rough-road winter-rally car was let down by a lack of straight-line performance. Already almost obsolete, it would soon be replaced by the much larger 2-litre 99 model.

engineered into a three-door hatchback bodyshell. Though Peugeot owned the business from late 1978, the Sunbeam-Lotus would be developed and campaigned in World Rallies by the Chrysler–UK team, based in Coventry.

In this case, the hatchback was the Talbot Sunbeam (which was itself on a shortened-wheelbase version of the Chrysler Avenger of the period), the engine being pure 16-valve Lotus, the gearbox a five-speed ZF like that of the Escort. Announced in 1979, and immediately competitive, it would be used until the end of 1981. Henri Toivonen used one to win the British RAC Rally in 1980, then in 1981 Talbot team would win the World Championship for Makes.

The programme would then be killed off by Peugeot, in favour of the Group B four-wheel drive Peugeot 205 T16.

its 16-valve engine at the end of 1977, and the extremely powerful Triumph TR7 V8 was only competitive on tarmac, even when the works cars could be persuaded to stay in one piece.

Compared with the 124 Abarth Rallye, how could the 131 Abarth be improved in the career which lay ahead? Since there was no way that further major changes could be made to the suspension and the traction without facing a completely fresh homologation run of road cars – and not even Fiat was ready to consider that – it could only be done by wringing every last scrap out of the existing conventional layout, and by making the latest cars as flexible as possible so that, theoretically at least, they would be more versatile than their competitors.

Homologation – meeting the rules

Fiat only ever intended the 131 Abarth to be a Group 4 car, so it therefore had to plan to build 400 examples and have them counted and/or approved by the authorities before their career in motorsport could begin. Like Ford, which had wrestled with the same dilemma in the late 1960s and early 1970s, Fiat's problem was not actually in the making of the cars – the will, the finance and the expertise were all available to ensure that – but where to make them?

The 131 family car range from which the new model evolved had been launched in October 1974, and by mid-1975 it was being manufactured in high numbers – thousands of cars every week – at Fiat's huge Mirafiori factory on the outskirts of Turin. Mirafiori was also the home of other Fiat mass-production models, and it would have been the height of economic lunacy to try to impose a short-run motorsport special on those regimented surroundings. Fiat's other plant, at Rivalta, also in Turin, was also unsuitable, so it was not long before it fell back on the safe, short-term manufacturing solution of having the cars partly-assembled outside Fiat to solve the problem.

Fortunately, there was a precedent. When Lancia (a Fiat-owned brand, don't forget) had faced up to the same problem in 1973 and 1974, it had also quailed at the complications before hiring the independent body manufacturer, Bertone,

Vauxhall Chevette HS – front-engine/rear-drive. This was Vauxhall's idea of a 'better Escort' – engineered in the same way, by slotting a powerful 2.3-litre engine and solid transmissions into a humdrum three-door hatchback bodyshell. Launched at the end of 1976, they were winners at British International level within six months. Then forcibly thrown out of motorsport for a time (because of homologation discrepancies) in 1978, the early works cars used Lotus instead of Vauxhall cylinder heads, along with a non-homologated back axle. When reinstated, they would not be competitive until 1979 – but could match up to most Fiats and Escorts after that. Better still in 1980, and onwards in HSR form, but this was when the Fiat was about to be retired.

Other makes and models also faced up to the 131 Abarth, but not consistently, or often enough. The Datsun 160J (2-litre, and otherwise a conventional car) was strong and competitive in rough events like the Safari, but rarely on tarmac, or in wintry conditions, Opel's Group 4 16-valve Asconas and Kadetts often suffered appalling reliability problems, and Peugeot's big 504 V6 Coupé was strictly an endurance/rough road/Safari type of contender, which never ventured into special stage rallies. Toyota's Celica dropped out of contention when new homologation rules outlawed

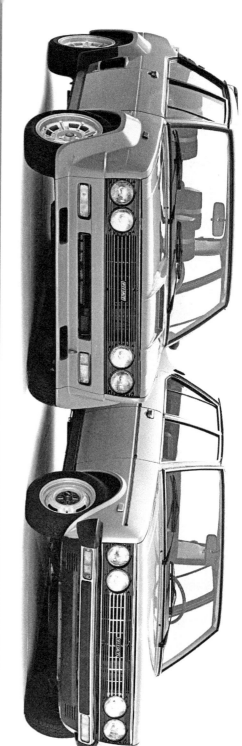

Before and after the Abarth treatment – on the right of the shot is the mass-production 131 saloon, while on the left is the 131 Abarth of which Bertone and Fiat would assemble 400 examples in 1975-1976.

The 131 Mirafiori from which the 131 Abarth was developed was a conventional Fiat family car intended for production in millions. The 131 Abarth, though, would be entirely different.

This was the 131 Abarth 'production car' of 1975-1976, of which exactly 400 examples would be built.

Seen on display at a motor show in Italy in 1976, this was the 131 Abarth which the public could buy. It was vastly different in every way from the 131 Mirafiori family car.

not only to engineer the Stratos structures, but to manufacture each and every one of the monocoques, before delivering them to a Lancia plant for final completion. And so it was arranged that, for the second time in three years, Bertone would come to the rescue in almost the same manner as before. Bodyshells would be constructed (using basic 131 two-door saloon structures, but of course heavily modified),

painted and trimmed on a special line in the Grugliasco factory on the outskirts of Turin, after which they would be trucked to the down-town Rivalta plant (where Fiat was already building 124 Spiders, Coupés and the last few 124 Abarth Rallye road cars) for completion.

Although it was already widely known to be under development, the first official press viewing of the car came

An early production-line 131 Abarth, newly built by Bertone and Fiat, is shown off to the press in January 1976.

in Monte Carlo, in January 1976. On the Monte Carlo Rally, Fiat showed an oven-ready example of the 131 Abarth, complete with the 'Olio Fiat' livery which would grace the original works cars. As already noted at the head of this section, this signalled the new management policy that in future, Fiat would compete in rallies with production-based cars while Lancia would eventually concentrate more and more on motor racing with prototypes. 131 final assembly, it was claimed, was already under way at Rivalta, there were no apparent problems with parts supply, and Group 4 homologation (which would place the new cars, head to head, against Lancia and Ford) was expected to come in the following month, February 1976.

Homologation, in fact, was not achieved quite as quickly as that – not even Fiat could always perform the smoke and mirrors trick of showing off non-existent cars to the FIA inspectors – but the authorities were finally convinced a few weeks later. According to the 131's Group 4 homologation form (No. 647), production had begun as early as 13 October 1975, and the 400th car had been completed before the end of March, which allowed homologation from 1 April 1976.

Weak jokes about 'April Fool' were made, of course, but Fiat took no notice of any of that, that Fulvio Bacchelli had already used an early car to win an Italian rally where homologation was not needed. The works team, led by Markku Alén, was avidly ready to start using the cars and immediately won the Elba Rally, and the first works cars appeared in a World event, in Morocco, a few weeks later.

By now experienced at this sort of thing, Fiat made sure that the 131 Homologation paper was a true work of art, an impressive document, 16 pages long, and full of technical facts (or, should I say, 'facts', for some of the items were definitely works-only material). Here are some examples:

• The 131 Abarth's weight, ready to roll, was quoted at 850kg/1874lb, which was a fictional figure. This was much lower than could ever be achieved on a rally car – even a tarmac rally car in 'lightweight' condition. The real unladen weight of road cars (which was quoted in authoritative directories of the period), was 980kg/2161lb.

• Three sets of intermediate gearbox ratios were quoted – the original 'road car' set, and two close-ratio sets which were intended for rallying use. This is a comparison of their internal ratios:

3.612, 2.045, 1.357, 1.000, 0.870, reverse 3.244
(this was the road car box)
2.156, 1.565, 1.242, 1.000, 0.802, reverse 2.666
2.021, 1.537, 1.185, 1.000, 0.876, reverse 2.666.

The 'road car' gearbox, in fact, was the same Fiat mass-production cluster as used in cars like the 131 and 132 family machines, though with synchromesh removed to meet the latest homologation regulations, while the 'competition' boxes were entirely different, their internals having been manufactured by CIMA in Bologna. To match these boxes, there was a big range of final drive ratios. The road car ratio was 3.90:1, the listed alternatives being 6.83, 6.42, 6.143, 5.375, 4.875, 4.625, 4.444, 4.30, and 3.63. Because their engine needed to be highly revved to get the most out of the car, and (in spite of its long-stroke layout) was lacking in lower-spec torque, rally cars tended to use the higher (numerical) ratios listed, but never those with 6.42 or higher, which were purely for sprint purposes.

• Fiat even went to the trouble of showing an illustration of the instrument layout of the rally cars, which would be significantly different from that of road cars.

Once the magic figure of 400 had been reached (and there seems to be little doubt that all the cars were actually built), Fiat and Bertone closed down the temporary assembly line, and apparently never re-opened it. As with the related Lancia Stratos, the 131 Abarth was built for a purpose, and built to meet a set of rules. Road cars, apparently, were sold on the basis that it was 'suggested' to every Fiat main dealer in Italy that, for patriotic purposes, they would be wise to take at least one car. In the provinces, apparently, many remained unsold for some time.

When those requirements had been met, Fiat pragmatically cut its losses (and, make no mistake, there had been a considerable financial 'investment' in this

A typical instrument panel of a 1977 specification works 131 Abarth.

131 Abarth bodyshells in series production at the Bertone factory, close to Turin, in 1976. Note the Fiat X1/9 assembly line in the background.

project which, translated, means that the programme was loss-making). In the years which followed, replacement and tune-up parts would be available in high numbers with high prices, as would two-door basic bodyshells – essentially the same as those of the bread-and-butter 131s – but complete new road cars were never made again.

From the outset, the works team at Abarth apparently reserved 50 modified bodyshells from the original build schedule of 400 cars, for its own use – and, indeed, a re-check of cars registered between 1976 and 1981 adds up to just that figure. However, in the late 1970s, when the need to lay down a small stock of replacement shells appeared, Abarth saw that the mass-market 131 had been given a front and rear-end styling makeover. Accordingly,

131 Abarth bodyshells were manufactured at this modern Bertone factory on the outskirts of Turin.

from 1 July 1978, a homologation amendment was made so that the latest shell, with different head and tail lamps, could be used for rebuilds.

Engineering features

The public's first sight of the car which linked the 131 road cars with the definitive 131 Abarth surfaced in October 1975, when works test driver Giorgio Pianta won the Giro d'Italia (Tour of Italy) in a two-door 131-based saloon called '131 Abarth.' This, though, was a very different car from those which would eventually go into rallying, for it had a 3.5-litre V6 engine which had been developed from the Fiat 130, a five-speed ZF gearbox in unit with the rear axle, monstrous wheelarch extensions and a massive rear aerofoil.

So far, so outrageous. But the important announcement made at the time was that a car developed from this base, would go into production with a 2-litre four-cylinder engine and thus: "... officially bring the 124 Spyder's career to an end." Although this was something of a smoke screen – the engine, the gearbox and the aerodynamic features would

This was the instrument display of the 131 Abarth road car – which would be radically changed for motorsport use.

Fiat issued a glossy brochure about the 131 Abarth when production cars went on sale. At speed, they looked impressive, though, as Ing. Sergio Limone has since revealed, they were by no means as completely developed as Abarth had hoped.

not figure on the production car – at least it alerted the media, and Fiat's rallying rivals, about the Italian company's intentions.

In 1975 Abarth's President was Aurelio Lampredi (ex-Ferrari engine designer), whose pride and joy was already the 124/125/131 engine range which he had inspired. The new rally car was designed completely by Abarth (only the engine – described below, came from Fiat itself), where Mario Colucci was the father of the 131 Abarth: he had recently moved across from Alfa Romeo. The chief test driver, quite pivotal to the entire project, was Giorgio Pianta. Although larger than, say, Ford's motorsport operation – the workforce totalled about 100 people – Abarth was a compact operation which could concentrate purely on this project. According to Ing. Limone, there were only six people in the design

offices at this time, three of them looking after power train work, the other three concentrating on chassis items.

Early decisions

For the analysis of the car, its engineering, and its development, I am deeply indebted to Ing. Sergio Limone, who not only worked on the 131 Abarth as a relatively junior engineer, but who was later responsible for the design of the Lancia Rally 037 and later Abarth products.

Ing. Limone told me that a very important early decision was made to choose an appropriate rear suspension: "When we started, we built several prototypes and tried different suspensions. One was with a rigid rear axle from the 132, rather like an Escort layout. One car had the 124 Abarth Rallye independent rear suspension. One was with the

29

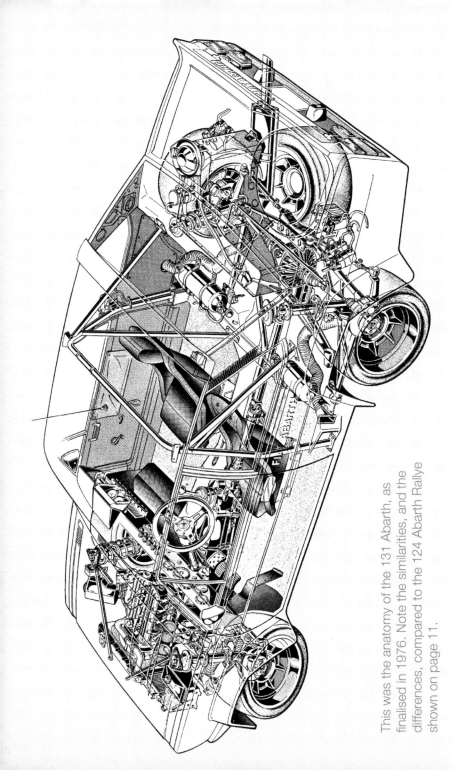

This was the anatomy of the 131 Abarth, as finalised in 1976. Note the similarities, and the differences, compared to the 124 Abarth Rallye shown on page 11.

X1/20 (Lancia Beta Monte Carlo) layout, one was with a new independent rear suspension we had just designed ourselves – and one was a De Dion axle so that we could keep the wheels upright. Immediately our choice was to use either the X1/20 layout, or the new Abarth layout. The Abarth layout was an improvement, but a big improvement, over the 124 Abarth Rallye system, because we had better control of the toe-in as it moved up and down. In fact, we chose our own new design – and the result was that the 131 Abarth always handled extremely well."

Once this big strategic decision had been made, the rest of the design followed logically from that. Limone, however, points out that the latest batch of Group 4 homologation rules,

which applied to all newly-homologated cars in 1976, banned the use of alternative cylinder heads, two-disc clutches, and non-synchromesh gearboxes unless all 400 homologation cars had similar fitments. This meant that the 16-valve engine would have to be productionised, and that for motorsport a new five-speed gearbox would have to be used.

Structure and layout

Fortunately, the 131 on which Abarth was told to direct its efforts was almost the ideal size and bulk for World Rallying. When launched as a mass-market car in October 1974, with a front engine and rear-wheel drive, it was a conventional

30

Fiat 131 Abarths did not have a rear bumper of any type. This car, which had been further tuned by Radbourne in the UK, was typical of the 400-off 'homologation run' built in 1975-1976

All 131 Abarths were fitted with rather squat, plastic wheelarch extensions to allow for ultra-wide wheels and tyres to be fitted. Note the air intake scoop, intended to channel fresh air to the rear brakes.

family car with a 98in wheelbase and a 166in overall length. With a monocoque shell constructed entirely from steel pressings, the mass-produced car was to be sold in two-door, four-door or five-door (estate) form, with push-rod overhead-valve engines, MacPherson strut independent front suspension, and beam axle rear suspension.

If that general layout sounds very familiar, that is because it lined up very closely with what the author calls the Ford Escort/Vauxhall Viva/Chevette and Opel Kadett template – this being what the marketplace seemed to expect in the mid-1970s. Almost by definition, this meant that for rally purposes, Abarth could 'build a better Escort', which it duly set out to do.

Naturally, Abarth chose the two-door version of the

The interior of the standard production 131 Abarth was elegantly trimmed; something of a waste on rally cars where all luxuries were ruthlessly stripped out!

131 road car shell, and set out to make it as light, but as strong, as possible. To accommodate and support the rear differential, it was only necessary to add a bracket and a vee-member to hold the diff. casing in place, this being one of the jobs done by Bertone when it was preparing the shell for production.

The skin panels of the car were all special to this model.

Front wings, bonnet panel and boot lid were all fashioned from glass-fibre (actually supplied by Cigala & Bertinetti, a Turin-based boat-building concern), and the wheel arch extensions were also in GRP: as homologated there were two different widths of extensions, the widest having to cover up to 10in front rims and 11in rear rims.

Door skins themselves were in aluminium, but the door

frames were in normal steel. Front and rear windows were in laminated glass, but side windows were in plastic. Aerodynamic add-ons included a roof deflector, a transverse rear spoiler on the boot lid, a special front spoiler with two brake cooling ducts, and in the rear wings there was also provision for cooling air for the rear brakes. The bonnet itself had a scoop on the left side, making extra provision to send cooling air into the engine intakes.

For obvious reasons, such a comprehensive reworking of the shell could only be done by a specialist company like Bertone, which took in near-standard partly-completed two-door shells from Mirafiori, and carried out the transformation on its premises in Turin.

There was no roll cage on the homologation cars – cages were not compulsory. Interestingly enough, the first generation of cars only used a part roll cage, with the main roll hoop immediately behind the passengers' heads, and with cross and other structural bracing behind that. The 1977 example, (a car originally driven by Markku Alén) displayed in Fiat's own Centro Storico, has just such a half roll cage. The full roll cage was added in later years.

Fiat and Abarth were always serious about the supply of special parts for the 131 Abarth competition car. This is how the plastic front and rear wing panels were marketed ...

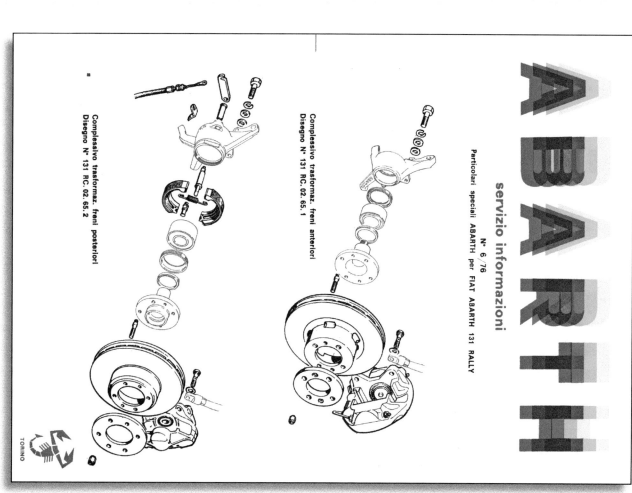

ABARTH

servizio informazioni

N° 6/76

Particolari speciali ABARTH per FIAT ABARTH 131 RALLY

Complessivo trasformaz. freni anteriori
Disegno N° 131 RC. 02. 65. 1

Complessivo trasformaz. freni posteriori
Disegno N° 131 RC. 02. 65. 2

TORINO

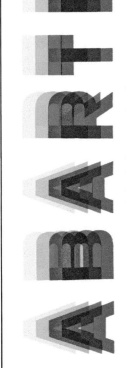

ABARTH

servizio informazioni

segue N° 6/76

Particolari speciali ABARTH per FIAT ABARTH 131 RALLY

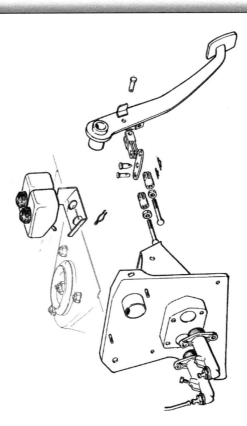

TORINO

Complessivo comando freni
Disegno N° 131 RC. 02. 68. 1

L'impianto frenante corsa comprende i dischi speciali autoventilanti, le pinze, le guarnizioni di attrito, e tutti i particolari differenti da quelli di serie e necessari per il montaggio.

Posteriormente l'impianto è dotato di freno di soccorso ad espansione completo di ceppi e tiranteria di comando.

La modifica è completata dal gruppo a doppia pompa di comando con vaschette ed impianti separati.

■ La potenza della frenata è regolabile rapidamente come ripartizione fra i due assi, mediante la adozione di differenti bilanceri di comando.

The 16-valve 2-litre engine fitted to the 131 Abarth was a snug fit into the engine bay. The brace across the engine was, of course, easily removable. This is a fuel-injected version of the power unit.

Engine

Although there were engineering links with the 16-valve engine of the 124 Abarth Rallye, the two types were different in many details, not least in cylinder head layout, and swept volume. Way back, however, both these engines were developments of the range of power units inspired by

Ing. Lampredi in the early 1960s. It's worth recalling the size of the ohv 1.6-litre engine used in the mass-market 131 road cars, and comparing this with the ultimate 124 Abarth Rallye (a 1.8-litre engine) and that chosen for the new 131 Abarth (which was a 2-litre unit):

As on other rival cars of the period – such as the Escort RS1800 – the boot of the 131 Abarth was well filled with battery (to the left), dry sump oil tank (centre) and the petrol filler and tank extension (right and centre). Somehow, space had been found for the spare wheel, too!

Engine	Capacity (cc)	Bore x stroke	Valves and valve gear (mm)
131 Road car	1585	84 x 71.5	2-per-cyl, overhead-valve (8 valve)
124 Abarth Rallye	1756	84 x 79.2	4-per-cyl, twin-overhead-cam (16-valve)
131 Abarth	1995	84 x 90	4-per-cyl, twin-overhead-cam (16-valve)

The typical layout of a works 131 Abarth engine bay, the 16-valve engine having fuel injection in fully-tuned guise.

Like the Ford Escort's celebrated BDA/BDG power unit, the 16-valve Fiat engine was loosely based on the bottom end of a sturdy mass-market pushrod overhead-valve engine, though with a cast iron rather than a cast aluminium cylinder block, the camshafts being driven by internally cogged belt. The same bore/stroke/engine size combination was already

used in an overhead-valve version, in the 132 production car – and would continue to be used by Abarth in even more specialised racing versions in future years.

It is immediately obvious that this engine would be heavier than the one fitted to, say, the Escort, and that because of its long-stroke layout, it would never be able to rev, nor to breathe, so freely. Although the torque delivery was promising, the crankshaft was heavy. Despite the fact that Abarth's engineers originally, and actively, wished to develop big bore/short stroke versions of this engine (a study of engine drawings suggested that this might just have been possible, though the block casting would have needed changes), this was eventually blocked by Ing. Lampredi. (In the 1980s, a modified 2.1-litre version was produced for use in the last of the Lancia Rally 037 cars.) Because Lampredi was so proud of the way that 'his' engine had evolved over the years, he was not willing (nor would Fiat sanction the time and expenditure involved) to go down this route, though five very promising experimental engines were indeed built and tested. All the work carried out (backed up by experience with the Escort hired from David Sutton) showed that even the ultimate Fiat engine could not match the Ford-Cosworth unit.

Although they looked superficially alike, the big difference been the 131 Abarth and the 124 Abarth Rallye engines was the 16-valve aluminium cylinder head itself. To make it easier to rebuild the engines, and to make them more suitable for a limited production run, the angle between the valves was increased (so that the cylinder head bolts could more easily be tightened, and thus the potential life of cylinder heads gaskets could be lengthened). On the 124 Abarth Rallye, it had been necessary to remove the camshafts themselves to gain access to the head bolts, which was not a satisfactory arrangement.

Along with the use of modified connecting rods, and bigger conrod bolts, the new head made the engine more durable. The production, 400-off, engine was fitted with a down-draught dual-choke Weber 34 ADF carburettor, and was rated at 140bhp at 6400rpm. Fully-tuned works rally engines used either twin vertical double-choke Weber 48 IDF carburettors, or (German) Kugelfischer fuel injection. Development work was also done using Spica fuel injection (Spica was a company owned by Alfa Romeo at the time, its injection system being used on several Italian cars destined for sale in the North American market), though this could not ultimately match up to the results gained on Kugelfischer.

Even so, and no matter how much effort was put in back at the Abarth workshops, this 16-valve engine was always at least 30bhp down on the Ford Escort power units, for it was rarely rated above 220bhp, and never above 230bhp.

Abarth always knew that the 131's engine would struggle against the opposition, so it made every attempt to produce the best engine for the best occasion. This explains why some engines had carburettors, and some fuel injection, and why different types of throttle control (Abarth slides in place of BMW Alpine butterflies), and a dry sump installation (homologated from 1 July 1977) were also developed. For the Safari, indeed, the engine was re-developed and slightly de-tuned to provide more low and mid-range torque. Sergio Limone comments that: "The drivers liked it so much that later they chose it for tarmac use also! The driveability was so much better that the drivers chose the Safari version."

Transmission

Fiat always planned to use a five-speed gearbox, but to meet the latest homologation rules (which applied from 1 January 1976) the road car boxes had to run without synchromesh, so that optional non-synchromesh boxes could be used in the works competition cars. To achieve this, what Ing. Limone has described as a 'horrible' road car gearbox was built in to the 400 homologation cars, with a reinforced 131 casing and dog-tooth engagement, but without synchromesh of any type. It was sometimes described as working like a lorry from the 1930s, and double declutching was always necessary. As far as is known, many road cars were later retrofitted with normal 131 synchromesh gearboxes, even though these were only marginally able to deal with the power of the homologation cars.

The clutch in the road car was a large diameter single-plate installation, derived from the Fiat Campagnola military vehicle. For competition use, Abarth (who had several experienced transmissions engineers) developed two new versions, the Tipo 165 with a direct fourth gear and an 'overdrive' fifth, along with the Tipo 168, with fifth gear being the direct ratio in that case. However, when the car was homologated in April 1976, it was offered with two

A worm's eye view of the rear suspension of a 131 Abarth, showing the way that the light alloy differential casing was supported by widely-spread mountings at the front, and how the rear suspension linked up to the diff behind its casing.

different types of 'overdrive' fifth gearboxes: the direct fifth gear installation was homologated from 1 January 1977.

Except in detail, the rear axle/differential (which was to be bolted up to the bodyshell – in-car refinement not being necessary!) was the same as that used in the earlier 124 Abarth Rallye. The casing itself was basically that of the Fiat 130 saloon/coupé, and the Fiat Dino 2400 model (which used the same basic rear suspension), though in aluminium rather than cast iron, but for the homologation cars the differential itself was that of the Fiat 241 commercial vehicle. Diffs used in works competition cars were extensively modified, and used ZF-type multi-plate limited-slip installations.

The road car used a 3.9:1 final drive ratio (to match up to the 'overdrive' fifth gear), but the homologation form included a mass of no fewer than ten different ratios, spanning 6.83:1 to 3.63:1. The lowest gearing (highest numerically, that is) was never needed in rallies, not even on events like the Tour de Corse. In most cases, it seems, the rally cars used 5.37:1 or 6.14:1. More ratios were added in the late 1970s.

Ing. Limone admits, candidly, that the performance of the rear drive shaft was the 'Achilles heel' of the installation, and that much development and strict 'lifing' on events was needed before Abarth finally adopted a new shaft based on

41

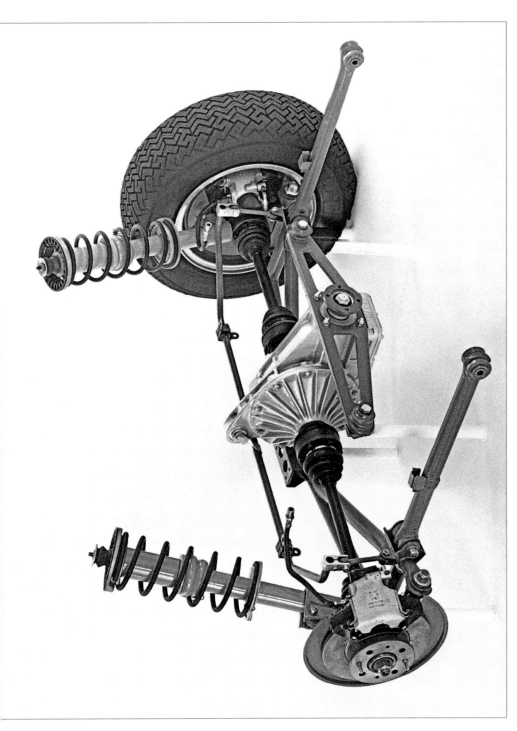

Beware – this is not a 131 Abarth rear suspension, but the slightly earlier 124 Abarth Rallye independent rear end. However, I have included it to show the general layout of the suspension geometry, and the bodyshell-mounted differential casing.

Suspension and brakes

Although the 131 Abarth was widely seen to handle better than the Escort, or even the Stratos (which could be a truly tricky beast to drive on bumpy terrain), this was not achieved without a great deal of hard work, development, and frustration for the design team. With MacPherson struts

that of the Lancia Stratos. Fiat, like Ford with the Escort, found that because of the constant jumping, along with loading and unloading of torsion stresses as the driven wheels left the ground, this imposed far higher actual torsional loads than calculations suggested should be the case!

42

Apart from the fact that the 131 Abarth struggled for grip on ice and snow (but what front engine/rear drive rally car did not?), it was an effective and photogenic works rally car on most surfaces. This testing shot was taken of a very early car in 1976.

fitted front and rear, and with a sophisticated rear end geometry, the basics were always right – it was the damping which gave so many problems, for there was a great deal of friction in the damper struts themselves.

Road cars were equipped with normal WayAssauto shock absorbers front and rear, while for the first two years the works rally cars used Corte & Cosso competition struts instead. Then, in something of a miracle cure, Walter Röhrl joined the team in mid-1977, tried a car, and told the engineers how unhappy he was with the damping. Ing. Limone and his boss, Mario Colucci, were both impressed: "Next time Walter flew in for testing, he had two sets of Bilstein dampers – four front and four rear – in his bags, and politely suggested, 'Try these …'. It was a revolution, the car was so much better." Almost at once, therefore, Abarth started talking to Bilstein's importer in Italy, supplies and settings were agreed, and the Germany company became a favourite supplier from then on.

Although the 131 Abarth's rear suspension linkage looks much like that of the 124 Abarth Rallye, there were many differences in detail and function. In particular, the tubular semi-trailing arms provided more accurate control of toe-in and toe-out settings, with later versions being reinforced to provide more strength on rough events such as the Safari and the Acropolis.

By comparing the homologation run with the works rally cars, the biggest compromise made on the grounds of cost and simplicity was with the brakes. While Abarth busied itself with the best and most functional four-disc layout for rallying, the cost-cutters imposed something much cheaper (and, frankly, nastier) on the homologation cars. At the front there were 227mm/8.9in discs, those of the Fiat 127, along with the brake calliper from that car, the same discs being used at the rear with callipers from the Fiat X1/9. Abarth thought this was all 'horrible,' but the system in the rally car itself was well-developed. Front discs were from the 130, with Porsche 911 aluminium ATE callipers, while at the rear there were special Brembo rotors and cast iron ATE callipers, all actuated by a Girling servo. Later in the life of the car, a complete Brembo system was also homologated, but never

extensively used. As with Ford's Escort, ways were found to use a 'hydraulic' handbrake too – this being displayed on the homologation papers.

Motorsport development and improvements

The early cars were by no means invincible, nor reliable, but determined work by Ing. Lampredi, Daniele Audetto, Nini Russo and their colleagues was always focused on making it so. The cars, which first appeared, in the European Championship Elba Rally of April 1976 still relied heavily on the chassis engineering of the 124 Spider Abarth. Quoted horsepower of the 2-litre engine was 210bhp at 7000rpm, which was not nearly enough for the cars to match up to Lancia (at home) or to Ford's Escort Mk IIs in World events. In Elba, all three cars used modified versions of the 131 Abarth road car gearbox, which was acknowledged to be weak, and would soon be supplanted by an Abarth-developed item. Two weeks later, gearboxes once again gave trouble on the Tulip Rally, and for a time there was panic in the ranks. Extra filters for the intake side of the engine reduced power to about 190bhp in Morocco, but the cars (like Ford's Mk II Escorts on the same event), wilted in the African heat, dust, and on the rocky stages.

In the early months, development of extra items continued apace. From July 1976, Fiat homologated a 'hydraulic handbrake' installation and a new type of skid cover underneath the rear differential, along with a variety of new brake parts, heavy-duty suspension castings, links and steering gear. Then, from 1 January 1977, the original ultra-close 'overdrive' set of gearbox ratios was replaced by a more sturdy set, with a direct fifth ratio set: 2.654, 1.895, 1.568, 1.244, 1.000, reverse 2.671.

During the winter of 1976-1977, much development work went ahead, not least with Pirelli, who would produce a bewildering and effective range of tyres – tarmac and loose surface, snow/ice or ultra-rough road – for its most important customer. The first fruits were seen in Monte Carlo, where the engines had 225bhp (still a lot less than their rivals), this being aided by a new exhaust system, which modified

TON19169 was an early 1975-1976 works 131 Abarth. The location is not known, but it seems that this was a cold-weather testing shot. Its attraction is that it is a perfect example of original 'Olio Fiat' livery.

and improved the engine's torque delivery. In the next few months, no more than detail retuning took place (including the use of extra-filter engines in New Zealand and the Acropolis), but in the Acropolis the team used the latest five-speed gearboxes with a direct fourth gear ratio, and an overdrive fifth ratio, along with more robust drive shafts.

By mid-season, too, much work had gone into making this car better on loose surfaces than on the tarmac for which it had originally been more suitable. Although there was no

difference in installation in the car, a major change which seems to have had an effect was to adopt German Bilstein dampers. This, as Ford had known for years, could make a great deal of difference to a car. At the same time, Fiat began to subscribe to the idea of having softer, longer-travel

Testing, testing … one of the standard press demonstration fleet at a proving ground in 1976. That is an Italian 'trade plate' which this car is carrying.

suspension off-road, which improved the traction. This process continued into 1978, the first fruit being a victory in Portugal.

For the engine, a dry sump installation had been tested earlier in the year, was homologated in mid-summer, and duly appeared on the 1977 1000 Lakes: reputedly this

gave an extra 10bhp by reducing 'churning' losses. The installation gradually took over on future events, though the transmissions – direct fifth or over-drive fifth – would be chosen to suit the particular events in question.

It was interesting to see that the Italian state-owned airline, Alitalia, which had previously been loyal to Lancia,

Testing of a Kugelfischer fuel-injected 131 Abarth at La Mandria proving ground in September 1980. From this angle, the use of plastic material in the bonnet panel is obvious.

began to apply the same livery to the 131 Abarth from the autumn of 1977 – another indication of the way that Lancia as a brand was now having to take a step backwards to let Fiat have every chance of victory and exposure.

Later in 1977, Fiat began to push the specification of the cars to the limit. Knowing that its engines could not match those of the Fords, it began to improve the power-weight ratio by reducing the cars' weight. On Sam Remo, for instance, the front wings were fitted ready-pigmented, instead of painted, while some elements of the roll cage were omitted: clearly this was only meant to be a 'tarmac car' specification.

For 1978 the specification appeared to have settled down. All engines, it seemed, now appeared with the slide-throttle inlet manifold arrangements which had been tried on various cars late in 1977, but with no more than 230bhp, their peak output still lagged significantly behind the output of the Ford Escort RS, still Fiat's major rival. Interestingly though, the company seemed much more bound up in re-branding the team than in making them faster and, with Lancia finally 'retiring' the Stratos, the Alitalia airline sponsorship livery, in vivid red, green and white, made many headlines on its own.

This was the season, however, in which Walter Röhrl's influence ensured that Bilstein dampers/struts would be used on the rally cars – there were two versions, a short one, with spacers, for tarmac, and a long one for rough-road/gravel events. In the same year, a new front suspension was refined, incorporating a forged aluminium lower arm. At the rear of the car, the introduction of Uniball bushes in the arms was a great advance over the hard rubber bushes which had originally been used.

At the end of 1978, Fiat admitted that its cars were no faster, in a straight line, than they had been all season – and it also admitted that the 16-valve 2-litre engines were stuck at no more than 230bhp, which was significantly down on that of its main rival, Ford, whose fabulous Cosworth-derived units were also more flexible, with more mid-range torque. By this time, though, the 131's handling had progressed so far as to be the very best of all contemporary rally cars, on any conceivable surface. It was team leader, Markku Alén, who had this to say in an end-of-year interview: "The car doesn't have the power. In a practice rally it's fantastic, when you know the corner. If you are driving blind, you hesitate, then there is no power after the corner. You watch on the special stages and you see the difference between the Ford and the Fiat. There was a much better chance to win [the RAC Rally] with the Stratos. Last year [1977] with the Fiat there was always a tyre problem – the compound was too heavy – and the suspension wasn't so good. Now we are using Bilstein suspension, and this is very good for asphalt and for loose. With the tyres and suspension we are getting better traction – the tyres aren't spinning."

From July 1978, minor homologation changes were needed to allow for the latest, different, rear light arrangement on what enthusiasts call 'Series II' cars, though this had no implications on the mechanical specification. At the same time, a further rear axle ratio (5.125:1) joined the impressive list of alternatives.

The works team spent much time early in 1979 preparing for its first visit to the Safari, with Sandro Munari apparently completing 20,000km in a variety of test and practice cars, which he progressively wore out! By Italian standards, these cars were positively heavyweight, all the works cars were new for the event, and all carried stout crash bars ahead of their headlamps and grilles.

By 1980, the pressure on the engineering team seemed to be off, as Ford had withdrawn from World Rallying and the 131 was already dominant. Since nothing could seemingly be done about the engines, which were no more powerful than they had been two years earlier, developments throughout the season were few, and concentrated on the two areas where work had already been needed – the transmission and the suspension. For the Acropolis Rally, ZF finally provided stronger differentials (Markku Alén having suffered badly with axle breakages in the past, and Fiat's patience finally snapped), and there was still much work going into the improvement of long travel/loose surface handling.

Late-model 131 Abarths sometimes appeared in

Many years after the cars had been retired, nicely-preserved examples – such as this ex-Walter Röhrl car – were still shown off at classic events.

all-tarmac/lightweight trim – notably on the Tour de Corse of 1980, where all three brand new cars were built in the same way. 'Lightweights' like these had small petrol tanks (homologated in July 1980, these had only a 50 litre/11 imperial gallon capacity), small dry sump oil tanks, lightweight front suspension arms, and much of the bodyshell stiffening was not present. Fiat claimed that this saved about 80kg/176lb, though because of the use of the small tank, it also admitted that the cars' fuel range was down to only 150km/93 miles. Woe betide any team whose 'top-up' planning at service points went awry!

Building and running the works cars

Although Fiat always seemed to build works cars in great profusion, the statistics prove otherwise – if, that is, you believe in vehicle registration numbers. According to irrefutable photographic evidence, between 1976 and 1981 (when the 131 was finally retired), Fiat entered just 45 works 131s at World level. This, in fact, was a very similar number to Ford, which prepared 33 Escort Mk IIs between 1975 and 1979 (plus five more cars from 'satellite' teams for the 1978 RAC Rally. As already noted, Abarth apparently reserved 50 shells from the production run of 400 homologation cars for

49

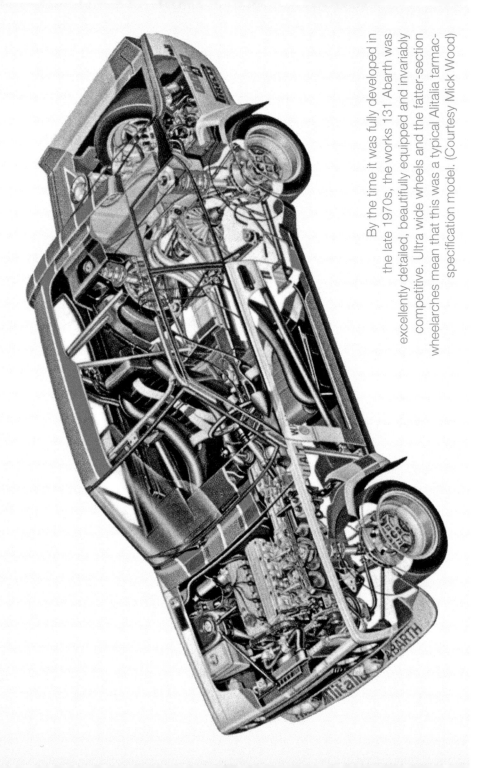

its own use, stored some of them for a while, but eventually used up the whole of that number just before the programme was finally wound up.

That is not to say that massive rebuilds were never tackled. Fiat, like Ford, certainly recycled cars (and registration numbers!) from time to time, for there is pictorial evidence to show that some comprehensively destroyed cars were miraculously re-born, and there is more that seems to show pristine 'new' cars carrying long-established, if not venerable, identities! Even so, it is worth pointing out that in 1977, when the Fiat 131 effort was building up to its peak,

no fewer than 20 all-new cars were created and rallied in World events – and this figure ignores any other machines which were only used in training, or testing.

Ace-tuner, Carlo Abarth, had sold his company to Fiat in 1971, and from the very early days the works 131 Abarth team was based at premises in north-west Turin in a building by no means as modern as the cars which it housed. Although ex-Ferrari engineer, Aurelio Lampredi, theoretically had much other work to do within Fiat, he was always involved in managing the effort, as was Daniele Audetto (before he was sent off to run the Ferrari F1 effort in 1976), while Ing.

Sileccia was team manager, and the seasoned race driver, Giorgio Pianta, provided an importance influence in the background.

Although Fiat had absorbed the financially-ailing Lancia company in 1969, in the early and mid-1970s the Fiat and Lancia motorsport operations considered themselves as rivals, not as colleagues. At the end of 1976, therefore, it was therefore something of a shock when top management decided to merge the two programmes, and house them in the same premises. From 1977, therefore, the hub of

Works 131 Abarth preparation inside the Abarth premises in 1977 – this Alitalia-liveried car appears brand new.

Model-makers and avid enthusiasts will need to study this 131 Abarth, one of the works cars to carry the Alitalia livery in the late 1970s. Neither the drivers' names nor the number plate panels have yet been added.

Fiat-Lancia's rallying operation was centralised at the Abarth plant at Corso Marche 38 on the north-western outskirts of Turin, a sprawling 11,000 square metre (120,000 square foot) complex of buildings on the edge of an airfield. For the next two or three years, privileged visitors could see 131 Abarths being prepared alongside Lancia Stratos types, though Stratos activity gradually faded away.

Once the Lancia and Fiat motorsport operations were

merged, Lancia's Cesare Fiorio became the overall chief, and the urbane Daniele Audetto became his on-event team manager who looked after whichever works cars (Fiat, or Lancia, or both) were competing. That relationship, incidentally, was often a little tense, for both could be described as prima donnas, and both needed to be supreme …

By any standards, Fiat had the world's biggest rallying

52

131 Abarth testing went on for years during the life of the project. This was Corsica in 1980, and an as-yet unregistered car.

budget in motorsport at the time. Ford, notoriously, was always starved of funds (which explains the amazing 'can-do' temperament which grew up around that team), so it was not until Mercedes-Benz, then Audi, got involved in World Rallying that Fiat's munificence was surpassed. It was Mercedes-Benz, in particular, that moved the goal posts as far as drivers' retainers were concerned.

When it came to preparing cars, Fiat never seemed to be short of space, or resources. Whereas the old premises always seemed to be somewhat cramped, and none-too-modern, the Abarth factory at Corso Marche was much more spacious. Providing cars for events never seemed to be a problem – Fiat (either under its own guise, or with additional cars loaned out to Fiat France) regularly entered four and even five cars for events held not too far from Italy, and a great deal of testing and development went on, helped by the fact that Fiat had its own test facilities not far away, as did Pirelli (who had a test track near Milan, just a couple of hours northeast up the autostrada).

It was a measure of Fiat's resources, and its determination to get to the pinnacle of the sport, that the team rallied no fewer than 13 new 131 Abarth rally cars in 1976 (the season did not begin, seriously, until homologation was achieved on 1 April), and followed this up by completing a further 20 new cars in 1977. It was an impressive fleet; works cars were rarely used more than three times before they were sold off, or were demoted to the status of training or engineering test cars, which explains why they usually looked absolutely immaculate when they turned up for pre-event scrutiny.

Due to the fact they had strong links with Alitalia in the mid and late 1970s, Fiat and Lancia were often able to arrange to fly cars to and from far-flung events, in one of Alitalia's capacious 747s, at very advantageous rates. Rivals like Ford found this difficult to do, as it had no good deals set up at the time.

Although Abarth made almost all the special parts available to private owners, to fashion a works replica was a very expensive business, and took a great deal of time. Abarth not only issued a leaflet advertising 'Ricambi' (parts), but there was also a list of the work necessary to complete a

state-of-the-art machine. Not only were the various features spelt out, but it was made clear that a 131 Abarth for forestry events for example, was different from hybrid cars, different again from lightweight/tarmac cars, and different yet again from the true heavyweights, built for the Safari and the Acropolis. Not only would there be major differences in wing mouldings and brake ducts, but more or less stiffening for the bodyshells. Add in the various permutations of brake specs, axle ratios and suspension changes, and the combinations seemed to be endless. For a team like Abarth, with a fleet of cars to choose from, this was acceptable, but private teams could only really afford to produce a compromise machine which was never really ideal for any use.

Just one aspect tells its own story – over the years, there were Cromadora magnesium road wheels, all of 15in diameter, but (depending on usage) with 5in, 7in, 8in, 9in, 10in and 11in rim widths.

Blind alleys

Although the 131 Abarth was a front-line works rally car for six eventful years, from time to time Abarth thought about replacing it, or producing different versions of the same car, but in all cases the finance and marketing staff inside Fiat stopped the projects. The two most important were:

Proposed Group 1 car – Jealous of the success of Ford's Escort RS2000, and of the Opel Kadett GT/E, both of which won hundreds of awards in the Group 1 'showroom' category, Abarth proposed its own particular type. To gain Group 1 status, 5000 would have had to be built on the mainstream assembly lines at the Mirafiori plant. Two prototypes were constructed, a steel-bodied 131 Abarth lookalike (complete with wheel-arch extensions), with the existing mass-production eight-valve twin-cam engine (as used in several Fiats and Lancias of the period), and the 131 Abarth-type independent rear suspension. It was a promising project, but was killed off when top management decided that it would have been too expensive.

V6 engined version – The Abarth 135 project was intended to be a faster, rarer and (by definition) more expensive evolution of the 131 Abarth. This featured a Fiat

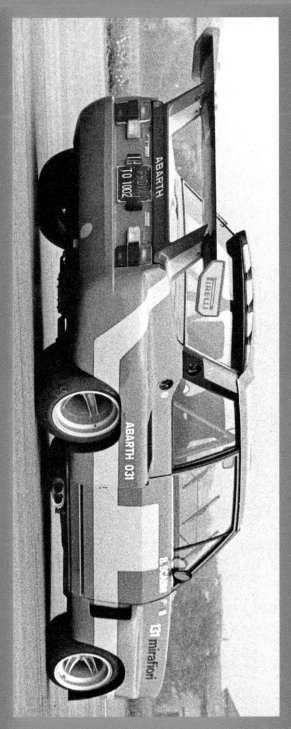

The very first Abarth-ised 131 was this V6-engined monster, which took part and won in the Giro d'Italia in 1975 with Abarth test driver, Giorgio Pianta, at the wheel. It was an inspiration to the 131 Abarth which followed, but by no means a direct ancestor.

This was the impressive line-up of drivers, managers and technicians involved in the works 131 Abarth rally team in 1976/1977. Among the many famous faces in the front row are Giorgio Pianta, Markku Alén, Simo Lampinen, Maurizio Verini, and Fulvio Bacchelli. Team Manager Daniele Audetto is on the extreme right in the back row.

130-type V6 engine up front (the very first prototype of a car like this was built in 1975, as I have already noted), with a five-speed ZF transaxle at the rear. Although every effort was made to turn this into a feasible project, it was cancelled when the prototype was found to be much too front-end heavy, which nothing could be done about.

Personalities and star drivers

Cesare Fiorio

Always a high-profile member of the Fiat and Lancia organisation, Cesare Fiorio ran that company's motorsport operations for 20 years before Lancia's owner, Fiat, promoted him to higher things. There is no doubt that Fiorio, along with his 'favourite son,' leading driver Sandro Munari, were the two major personalities who turned the

Stratos from 'Great Idea' to 'Great Car,' and it was Fiorio and his associate, Daniele Audetto, who made so much of the 131 Abarth. Only Fiorio, along with his father (who was Lancia's publicity chief in the 1970s) and Audetto, could have persuaded the company to spend so much money on motorsport.

Originally the Fiorio family had a leather business in Turin, but Cesare's father, Sandro, then broke with tradition by joining Lancia. Cesare, his son, first studied political science, then dabbled with racing and rallying, spent time in the Italian navy, joined a Lancia dealership, and was instrumental in setting up HF Squadra Corse.

From 1965 HF Squadra Corse became, de facto, the Lancia works team, and from that time Cesare Fiorio devoted all his efforts to promoting and expanding the team. First with Flavia Coupés, then with Fulvia Coupés, and then the Fulvia 1600HF, Fiorio wrung more money out of his bosses, hired superstar drivers, and turned Lancia into a formidable race and rally team.

It was Fiorio who inspired the birth of the Stratos and directed its career, but he was also involved in the Fiat rally programme until the parent company decided to merge the Lancia and Fiat motorsport operations. After this, he then directed the merged team, though much of the day-to-day management was delegated to Daniele Audetto, for Fiorio was very involved in directing Lancia's major involvement in sports car racing. He still found time to go powerboat racing at the weekend, however!

By 1981 the Lancia Rally 037 was conceived (as Fiat-Lancia's first Group B Rally car), Fiorio was promoted yet again, and, after Fiat took over Alfa Romeo in 1986, he added that responsibility to his portfolio. There was more to come, for he became Ferrari's sporting director in 1989, was ousted in 1991, then moved in and out of other F1 teams for the rest of the decade.

Smooth, sophisticated, and a real behind-the-scenes wheeler/dealer/ fixer, he was sometimes unkindly

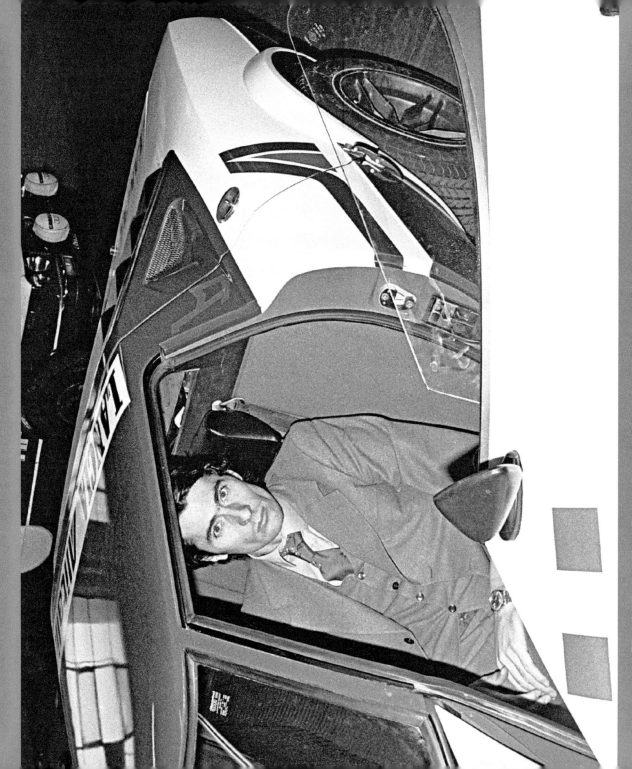

Daniele Audetto was Fiat's ruthlessly capable Team Manager in the World Rally programme.

called 'Mr Hollywood' because of his perma-tan and his liking for the high life. Nevertheless, he should always be remembered for the great things his Lancia and Fiat teams achieved in the 1960s, 1970s and 1980s.

Daniele Audetto

By any standards, even by Italian sartorial standards, Daniele Audetto was 'Mr Smooth', the ultra-cool, softly spoken and ever-so-sophisticated team boss of the Fiat motorsport team in the high-profile days of the 131 Abarth. When all around him were either sweaty or drenched in the rain, Audetto somehow would remain smart, even if casually dressed. Many envied him, not only for that, but also for the way that his mind could work around the machinations of homologation, of team management, and of pure rally-craft.

Like many others in the rallying business, he started out in the sport as a competitor, but moved on to management, and later to even higher things. Born in Turin in 1943, the young Audetto began his working life as an artist and journalist and took up rallying as a co-driver (two of 'his' drivers at Lancia were Luca di Montezemolo and Sandro Munari, which made him extremely well-connected). Suffering badly injured legs in a rallying accident, he retired and took up management within the Fiat group instead, and, under Cesare Fiorio, was Lancia's team manager in the early years of the Stratos. From 1976, however, Luca di Montezemolo moved out of his job at Ferrari, and installed Audetto as team manager in his place. He oversaw the F1 team's activities in 1976 and early 1977, and was then moved to run the Fiat rallying operation. It was under Audetto that the 131 Abarth won its Manufacturers' Championships in 1977, 1978 and 1980.

Then in the early 1980s, he moved away from Fiat-Lancia (apparently there had been another difference of opinion with his boss, Cesare Fiorio), and in the next 20 years moved into higher and higher positions with Lamborghini, in the World Superbike Championship, in Ligier and in Arrows. When this book was originally being researched in 2007, he had become Managing Director of the Super Aguri F1 team.

This great, and much respected, engineer was already famous for his work at Ferrari before he moved to Fiat, and would later be the top man at Abarth. It was under his control that the 131 Abarth was designed, developed, and campaigned in rallying.

Ing. Lampredi

Born in 1917, Aurelio Lampredi began his career in the naval shipyards at Livorno before working on aircraft engines at Piaggio. He then moved to work for Isotta-Fraschini, and spent Italy's war years designing fighting aircraft at Le Reggiane, near Modena. Immediately after the war, Lampredi joined Ferrari. He then moved back to Isotta Fraschini, to work on the rear-engined Monterosa model (which was stillborn), before returning to Ferrari. There he made many refinements to the small supercharged vee-12, before producing the first big vee-12 GP engine for which he became famous – this being the 4.5-litre unit which brought Ferrari its first World Championship F1 victories. Enzo Ferrari, they say, was not best pleased that an 'outsider' should be credited with this work. Even so, Lampredi survived at Ferrari until 1955, but after the entire F1 Lancia effort had been handed over to Ferrari (including Lancia engineer, Vittorio Jano), he was soon ousted.

Fiat technical chief, Dante Giacosa, then hired him to oversee the Fiat engine design team. Among many new engines produced were the famous twin-cam 124/125 power units (which would eventually give rise to the 16-valve 131 Abarth engines), the production versions of the Ferrari Dino V6 (which powered the Lancia Stratos), and an entirely different big Vee-6, which was used in the Fiat 130.

Towards the end of his career, Lampredi moved from Fiat's HQ, to be the Managing Director of the Abarth business, running it from 1973 to 1982, the period that includes all the successes of the 131 Abarth.

Markku Alén

'Maximum attack' is a phrase which is ideally applied to the lanky Finn – and it was one which he used often. Compared with easy stylists like team-mate, Walter Röhrl, Markku's driving style was urgent, sometimes brutally direct, and always flamboyantly exciting to watch. In almost every way, except for the definition on his passport, Markku was an archetypal 'Latin', who lived up to his reputation at all times.

By any standards, Markku was the longest-lasting star of the front-line Fiat-Lancia works teams, for he first drove a works car (a 124 Spider Abarth) in March 1974, and his last drive (in a Lancia Delta Integrale) came in Australia in September 1989. From start to finish he was a favourite with rally fans all around the world, as flamboyant as he was fast – and always competitive.

Born in Helsinki in 1951, Markku started rallying in a Renault 8 Gordini. On his very first World Rally – 1000 Lakes 1973 – he took second place in a Volvo 142, was snapped up by Fiat for 1974, and won his first World event, in a 124 Spider Abarth, in Portugal in 1975. From then on, he was always a leading light in the Fiat team, occasionally getting an outing in a Lancia Stratos, before moving smoothly across to driving Lancia Rally 037s, Delta S4s and Delta Integrales.

Not only did Markku give the 131 Abarth its first World win – 1000 Lakes 1976 – but its last one too – Portugal 1981. All in all he won eight times, in 131 Abarths, and was never less than competitive. Along with Walter Röhrl (see below) he was the driver whose wishes were incorporated as closely as possible. Markku, being Markku, could be very demanding, very dismissive of the team's efforts if it did not match up to his own expectations – but no-one ever tried harder to win an event.

After moving on from Fiat-Lancia, Markku then drove Subaru and Toyota cars. In an astonishingly successful rally career, which did not end at World level until 1993, he won no fewer than 20 World events, though the accolade of World Champion just eluded him on several occasions.

Markku Alén (right) and his co-driver, Ilka Kivimaki, formed the single most successful crew to drive the 131 Abarth.

Markku Alén of Finland was not only a favourite with the crowds, but also one of the most formidable of a stellar line-up of drivers in the 131 Abarth works team.

Walter Röhrl

Although the speed and capability of both Markku Alén and Walter Röhrl was never in doubt, the difference between the two drivers was marked. Whereas Alén was all heart, all passion, and all arms, legs and elbows, Röhrl was always cool – glacially so, in truth – clinically exact in everything he did in a motor car, and quite amazingly effective. A German, formal, correct, efficient, and never satisfied with less than his best, Röhrl was a stunningly successful driver for ten years. Abarth personality, Sergio Limone, once described Röhrl's driving style as " … like going out for a Sunday afternoon spin with Grandma … ", so easy and precise was his method.

Right from the start of a glittering career, Röhrl's eventual success as a World Champion never looked to be in doubt – though the vicissitudes of his early employer's Opels made it difficult to see how that would happen. Born in Regensburg in 1947, he started World Rallying in Opels in 1973, won for the first time in Greece in 1975, but did not become a consistent winner until he joined Fiat full-time in 1978. It was only after this that his amazingly consistent results began to build up.

Röhrl's victory in six World Rallies for Fiat was just one of his many achievements. He won the Monte Carlo Rally four times in succession – in 1980, 1982, 1983 and 1984 – a feat which has never been matched by anyone else, and incidentally each of those wins was in a different make

Walter Röhrl (far left) talks to Daniele Audetto at a service point on the 1978 Burmah Rally (held in Scotland). Röhrl was on his way to fourth overall.

and model of car. After his sojourn with Fiat, Röhrl drove successive seasons with Opel, Lancia, and Audi (with the Quattro). He later won events like the Pike's Peak hill climb, and was close to Audi until the early 1990s, after which he took up a senior testing job with Porsche. Röhrl was World Rally Champion in 1980 and 1982.

Bernard Darniche

Although Frenchman Bernard Darniche only won two World Championship Rallies in Fiat 131 Abarths, he was also a formidable competitor at European and French Championship levels. His two victories, in any case, were in that most formidable event of all – the Tour de Corse.

Darniche began his works rallying career in Alpine-Renault A110s in 1973, and was always at the top of the listings for a decade. His first works drives for Fiat were in 1974 (124 Abarth Rallye), after which he went on to join Fiat-Lancia in 1975, becoming team leader of the Fiat France team and later of Team Chardonnet (the importer of Fiats into France).

Between 1975 and 1981, most of Darniche's successes were recorded in Lancia Stratos two-seaters, for which he rightly became famous, but in a two-car team (Mmle Michèle Mouton was the other regular driver) he was always competitive in 131 Abarths. These cars, incidentally, were always supplied by Abarth, either as newly-built machines, or as 'young' ex-works cars which had been sold off after two or three events.

Among rally fans, Darniche is famous for winning on the very first occasion he drove a works 131 Abarth – and also for coming to terms with his balding pate by suddenly doing a deal with a French toupee manufacturer, and subsequently appearing with a full head of hair! All in all, he won seven World Rallies, driving not only the 131 Abarth, but also Lancia Stratos and Alpine-Renault A110 types.

Competition story

The competition programme for the 131 Abarth took shape as briskly, as purposefully, and as logically as it had begun. With the new car launched early in 1976, and with homologation achieved in April a few months later, it was immediately pronounced ready to take over from the ageing 124 Abarth Rallye. It was entered in the Elba Rally, a European Championship qualifier, and recorded a 1-2 finish. Fiat was then brave enough to enter cars in the rough and demanding Rally of Morocco (it won the 1000 Lakes Rally in August), and a glittering career began to unfold. This, in every way, was a perfect example of how to launch, develop and campaign a rally car.

1976

It was a measure of how significant the 131 Abarth's debut seemed to be that Britain's *Autosport* magazine devoted three pages to reporting on Elba which, by its normal reporting standards, was an obscure European event. Fiat sent along three brand new 131 Abarths, decked out in what was to become a familiar Olio-Fiat livery, to be driven by Markku Alén, Fulvio Bacchelli and Maurizio Verini.

Although the principal opposition came from Mauro Pregliasco's works Lancia Stratos, and Stig Blomqvist's 16-valve Saab 99, the main interest was in seeing if the new car looked competitive, and would last the distance of a two-day event on tarmac and some gravel stages. In the end the 131s finished first (Alén) and second (Bacchelli), though the third car retired with gearbox failure. The bad news was

Picture of a happy man! Markku Alén in his native Finland in 1976, when he gave the car its first World victory.

that both surviving cars needed complete gearbox changes to keep them going, and it was only the lack of credible opposition (the Stratos and the Saab both retired) which allowed them to win at all.

However, as all the best beleaguered managers always say, "A win is a win" – Fiat went back to Turin, put in more determined development work, and got the cars ready for their first World Championship round. Amazingly, it entered three new cars in the rough, tough and dauntingly extreme Rally of Morocco, though with engines de-tuned to only 190bhp (extra filtration systems ahead of the fuel-injection installation didn't help) the cars were less competitive. Although the 131s lead the rally for some hours, two of them eventually retired – one with a broken differential, the other with deranged suspension caused by the battering received by the damper bolts, but the gritty Alén kept on going through every problem, and eventually finished 12th, many hours behind the winning Peugeot 504s.

Suddenly, in August 1976, it all came together for the team as Markku Alén, determined to win in his native Finland, took another brand new car to Scandinavia and won the 1000 Lakes in a storming drive, defeating everything that Ford, Saab, Toyota and Datsun could throw at him. And it was a convincing win too, for he recorded 18 fastest stage times (more than anyone else), and won by 45 seconds. Apart from the fact that a sparkplug broke up under the strain at one point (and was thought to have damaged a piston), the car behaved faultlessly, and frightened all its opposition with its potential. This had been a remarkable performance on what was only the car's second World Rally.

It was too much to expect, however, that a repeat performance on home ground in San Remo would follow, and it did not. The record shows that the in-house rival, Lancia's Stratos, took the top four places, while all four works 131s retired. Two of them – driven by Alén and Bacchelli – crashed, and one suffered an electrical then a differential failure. Verini's car, which lasted longest, was competitive with the Lancias, which was at least a promising portent for the future.

Fiat, perhaps wisely, then decided to ignore the Tour de Corse, where twisty stages were always likely to over-stress the transmissions, and instead sent three cars to tackle the British RAC Rally instead. Although Fulvio Bacchelli finished 11th, he and his car were quite outclassed by the squadrons of secret-stage forest-specialists who flocked to this rally. At one point Alén was as high as fourth, but his car suffered many punctures and a broken crown wheel and pinion, and Verini's car succumbed to a broken gearbox. Clearly Fiat would have to address the transmission frailties, and solve them in the coming winter.

1977

Suddenly, and seemingly from nowhere, Fiat had honed the 131 Abarth into a World-Championship winning motor car. In the first year the works cars had struggled for reliability, now, in 1977, they became formidable standard-setters. Having spent the first season sorting out the basic specification of the 131s, Fiat then threw all its effort behind the development of the cars in the winter of 1976-1977, and was so successful that it won the first of three World Championship for Makes prizes in the season which followed.

Not only did team cars turn up on all but one of the eleven Championship rounds – a series which spread its wings, and included a rally in New Zealand and one in Canada, too – but they recorded five outright victories, and were always on the pace. As has already been noted, the company was now concentrating on the 131 Abarth at the expense of the charismatic Stratos.

With this in mind, not only would four 131 team cars (with Alén, Verini and Bacchelli as core members, though Simo Lampinen, and Jean-Claude Andruet's Fiat France car also joined in at times) be entered on many events, but parts, equipment and expertise would be made available to Fiat importers in other countries. This was going to need a large fleet of new cars, which were duly prepared – and, as the author's research has shown, at least twenty brand new machines were built, while some of the nine existing cars from 1976 were also retained.

The 131's first attempt at the Monte Carlo Rally came in 1977 and was very successful. This was Jean-Claude Andruet's Fiat France entry, which finished a dutiful second behind Sandro Munari's works Lancia Stratos.

Four cars started in Monte Carlo, and the result – second place for Andruet, just 2 minutes 16 seconds behind Sandro Munari's Lancia Stratos – was the very best which could be expected. Although Alén was consistently faster than Andruet (and had to be restrained from attacking the Stratos's position at times!), his car suffered two catastrophic electrical failures, which finally caused him to retire. Both Verini (in a crash) and Bacchelli (a crash, then half-shaft failure) also retired.

Alén, Timo Mäkinen (newly ex-Ford) and Simo Lampinen started in Sweden, but once again it was reliability, not pace, which was lacking. Alén's car gave repeated electrical trouble, then burnt out after a fuel pipe came adrift in the engine bay, Mäkinen held second place for a long time before the rotor arm in his engine's distributor failed, and in the end it was Lampinen (a Finn who had driven for many teams, including Lancia, in the past) who took second place behind Stig Blomqvist's front-wheel drive Saab 99EMS.

The first victory of the year was now overdue, and finally arrived in Portugal, where Markku Alén fought a titanic battle with Björn Waldegård's works Ford Escort RS1800. The usual three front-line drivers started the event, along with Andruet in his Fiat France car. Amazingly, on this 46-stage rough-and-tough event, three Fiats finished first, fourth (Andruet) and fifth (Verini): only Bacchelli dropped away

66

Maurizio Verini enjoyed works drives for both Fiat and Lancia in the late 1970s, but was not the luckiest of drivers. Here he was on his way to fifth place in Portugal in 1977.

after his 131 suffered from damaged rear suspension which took a long time to repair.

The 131 Abarth was now moving rapidly towards maturity, for as *Autosport's* Rallies Editor, Peter Newton, commented after that famous victory: "The 131s, with their excellent balance and stabilising understeer, handle superbly on tarmac, and it was expected before the rally that they would easily out-distance the Fords on the comparatively few asphalt tests ..."

This, indeed, is how the Italian car's career would progress in the future. A 20-30bhp power deficiency over the Escorts and the Lancias would never be made up, but this was usually balanced by the superior sealed-surface handling (and the bigger budget!) it always enjoyed.

Wisely, in most people's opinion, Fiat then avoided the Safari (one which Lancia had hoped to win in the Stratos, but narrowly failed) before sending a team to New Zealand to compete in the South Pacific event. Amazingly, the 131 then notched up its second consecutive victory, though it surely did not deserve it, as the cars only recorded 19 fastest stage times compared with 47 for Ari Vatanen in an Escort RS1800. Here, though, was a thoroughly professional performance on an event which the Italians had never tackled before. Alén, Bacchelli and Lampinen drove the Fiats, all of them squaring up against Ari Vatanen in a New Zealand-prepared RS1800. Although Vatanen was the quickest

Parc Ferme line-up of leading cars in Portugal in 1977. Marku Alén's 131 Abarth, closest to the camera, would win, Ove Andersson's Toyota would take third, and Björn Waldegård's Ford Escort would take second place.

driver in the country that weekend, he had not just one but three time-consuming crashes (at one point he lost 23 minutes in a stage!).

The 131s, for their part, all had major problems to sort out, including an engine oil leak in Alén's car, an 'off' for

Bacchelli, who was leading at the time, and delays while other team cars helped Bacchelli get his car back on to the road. On the last day, the engine in Bacchelli's car began to sound very sick indeed, most of the oil pressure was lost, the oil pump had to be changed, and in the end the 131

though Fiat sales in New Zealand itself were very limited, top management in Turin were relieved to recoup some of their considerable investment.

The team effort which followed in the Greek Acropolis Rally, if not quite as expensive, was equally as instructive. In an event where success would tell the rallying world so much about the rugged worth of its latest design, Fiat, having carried out much pre-event testing to make sure that the engines were dust proof, entered (or supported) no fewer than six of the latest-specification cars.

Compared with its recent successes in Portugal and New Zealand, this was a rally where Fiat struggled, for nothing could compete with Ford's fast and rugged Escort RS1800s, and the best that Turin could achieve was fourth by Simo Lampinen. Of the other cars, every single example eventually retired with a broken drive shaft – so these were obviously not as strong as they had been claimed to be before the start! Not even Markku Alén could set fastest times – in the whole event Fiat only set two, by Lampinen, in his old-specification car.

Fiat now knew that it had a fight on its hands, for Ford (having won the Safari and Acropolis Rallies) announced that it had found extra funds, and would tackle every World Rally in the remainder of the year. What followed was a classic head-to-head fight, which would only be settled when Ford's effort failed in San Remo.

In Finland (the 1000 Lakes) at the end of August, it was Ford whose Escort once again won, and the only Fiat to finish strongly was that of team newcomer, Timo Salonen, who took second place. Fiat actually brought along five 131 Abarths for this occasion, but it was only Markku Alén who was able to match the pace of Ford's Kyosti Hamalainen. Unhappily for Alén, who led the rally at half distance, his 131 hit a large rock which appeared to have been put in place in the landing zone of a high-speed 'yump', resulting in a smash which wiped off the sump guard, the engine oil pump, two wheels and much of the suspension. Although his mechanics somehow cobbled the car together again, before long the engine objected to this and blew in the biggest possible way. It was not until Björn Waldegård hit

Fulvio Bacchelli, who had risen to stardom driving the 124 Abarth Rallye, won the South Pacific (New Zealand) Rally of 1977 in this 131 Abarth.

staggered across the ramp with a three-cylinder engine! Fiat, of course, was delighted by the expensive, but ultimately successful outing, for the team cars had taken first, third and fourth places – only the amazingly lucky Vatanen had stopped Fiat recording a remarkable 1-2-3 result. Even

After spending thousands of hours in testing, Fiat made the 131 Abarth into a car which handled well on all surfaces – this being Simo Lampinen, sideways, on his way to second place in Canada in 1977.

a similar obstacle in the 1979 Monte that such a scandal repeated itself.

With Ford now six points ahead of Fiat in the World Championship, both teams sent cars to the Canadian Rally of Quebec, where the stages would be long and very fast. Two Escorts were matched by no fewer than five 131s,

driven by Alén, Lampinen, Salonen, Walter Röhrl (who had been poached from Opel) and Timo Mäkinen, a stellar line-up by any standards.

Although the 131's engines were still sometimes fragile – Röhrl, Alén and Mäkinen all retired with engine blow-ups – two other 'team Finns', Timo Salonen and Simo Lampinen, kept going strongly to the end. Luck was with them, for a Ford victory seemed assured until Vatanen's engine let go towards the finish, and Salonen won his first-ever World event, indeed his first-ever victory outside his native Finland. Roger Clark (Escort RS1800) took a rather disheartened third place.

Fiat still lagged behind Ford in the World series, though, so another major effort followed, on home ground in the San Remo. This time there was no mistake. No fewer than six brand new factory-supported 131s took the start (the 'A-Team' from Turin being driven by Bacchelli, Röhrl and Verini – though, surprisingly, not Markku Alén), two others

Not only was Markku Alén the most successful driver in 131 Abarths, but he was always the most popular with spectators. Quebec, 1977.

were provided for Tony Fassina and Livio Lorenzelli, and Andruet had one of his usual Fiat France cars.

This was no demonstration run, as four Lancia Stratos cars also started (having been prepared in the same workshops!). The battle was long and hard (*Autosport's* report was headlined 'Family at War'), but in the end, only

one Stratos (Pregliasco's car) made it to the finish, while Fiat Andruet took 1-2-3 (Andruet, Verini and Fassina). Ford's major effort was a huge disappointment – Waldegård was fifth – and suddenly Fiat was once again in the lead for the World Championship.

With four victories and two second places already

The colour scheme may be unfamiliar, but success in the San Remo Rally was not. This was 1977, when Jean-Claude Andruet used his Fiat France car to take outright victory.

In 1977, Fiat and Lancia were operating as one motorsport organisation. This was the Tour de Corse in 1977, with Raffaele Pinto's Alitalia-liveried Stratos alongside Bacchelli's 131 Abarth, which finished third.

recorded, Fiat fans now expected a further victory in Corsica a few weeks later – and this was duly delivered. Once again, Ford's effort was a huge disappointment (both highly-tuned Escorts retired), but Fiat produced a storming result, notching up first, third and fifth places (with two Lancia Stratoses breaking up the squadron finish).

Operating not far from home base, of course, Fiat had practiced diligently, and entered Olio Fiat cars for Röhrl, Bernard Darniche, Bacchelli and Verini, while Fiat France entered cars for Andruet, Francis Vincent, and a young lady called Michèle Mouton who was in her first-ever drive in a 131. In fact, Röhrl did not start, for he was reputedly

Fiat made occasional forays into British rallies, but could never quite match the pace of the works Escorts. This was guest-driver Billy Coleman in the Pirelli-sponsored Chequered Flag works car, on his way to fourth in Scotland in 1977.

still nursing a wrist injury sustained on a previous event. Although Lancia was originally expected to win (despite the fact that the cars had been prepared in the same cavernous workshops in Turin, there were, apparently, no team orders), fate was against it. Munari, of all people, went off the road, Pinto's car was as fast as Darniche's winning 131, but also went off the road for more than three minutes, and Fiat's massive service back-up just tipped the balance. At the end of the day, and after 13 amazingly serpentine stages, Darniche beat Pinto's Lancia by more than three minutes –

the same three minutes, it seemed, as Pinto had lost in that single accident.

Fiat was in seventh heaven, as the loss of the Fords meant that the Italian team had now won the World Makes Championship for the first time – and the corporate decision to concentrate on Fiat, at the expense of Lancia, had demonstrably paid off.

Although there was no need for the 131s to enter Britain's RAC Rally, Fiat at least took it all seriously and did the honourable thing. Having sent an old car to tackle the

1978

Castrol 77 (national) Rally in Wales (where Markku Alén finished third), it was more confident than in 1976, and sent no fewer than six cars to tackle the event. This was almost an end-of-season clear out, for three of them were full Olio Fiat-sponsored entries, and three more were jointly sponsored with Graham Warner's Chequered Flag operation in London. All the usual names were present, though it was the Scandinavians – Markku Alén, Lampinen, Salonen and Timo Mäkinen – who were expected to set the pace.

Fiat's suspicion that it could not match Ford's Escorts was soon confirmed, and not even Alén could match the pace of Björn Waldegård in his RS1800. At the end of a long, gruelling, and tough event, Lampinen's car took seventh place, and all the other 131s wilted. Accidents, engine failures and multiple punctures accounted for the rest: even Timo Mäkinen (11th) went off the road for ten minutes at one point. All in all, this was a very downbeat way to end a spectacularly successful season.

In order to learn more about the 131 Abarth's abilities in British forests, Abarth loaned a car to the Chequered Flag (who was already running a Lancia Stratos) in 1977. This car – TON 94415 – had already been driven by Markku Alén in the 1976 RAC Rally. Driven by Billy Coleman and David Richards on the Welsh, it not only broke a gearbox, but had unsuitable tyres (so Fiat was, at least, learning something!), and went off the road for a time. Weeks later, and after a complete rebuild, the same crew tackled the Scottish and finished fourth, behind two factory-specification Escort RS1800s and Tony Pond's Triumph TR7. Fiat took this little programme seriously – both Ing. Colucci, and Sergio Limone attended events to observe – but it was not ultimately successful.

Although Fiat then set out to repeat its World Championship success in 1978 – something which it would, indeed, achieve after a huge effort – its season began badly, with something approaching a shambolic performance in the Monte Carlo Rally. Perhaps some of this can be blamed on the weather, but the fact is that it became the only Monte in the modern era to be won by a private car (and an obsolete-type private car at that – Jean-Pierre Nicolas's Porsche 911). Worse, in Fiat's stellar team, only the new regular, Walter Röhrl, really shone on the ice and snow. Perhaps Fiat would have been more fortunate if Verini had not spun his 131 between snow banks in the Col de Perty stage, got it stuck, and not only

Fiat promises to forget the shambles of its 1978 Monte Carlo efforts if you will. All team cars suffered from hold-ups on blocked stages, and a poor choice of tyres didn't help either. Car No.8 was driven by Bernard Darniche, who finished fifth.

A tarmac-specification, Alitalia-liveried 131 Abarth from 1978, as driven by Walter Röhrl, on display twenty years later looking just as good as new. (Courtesy Mick Wood)

suffered a major time loss himself, but held up all his team mates in the process!

Despite the fact that its cars could not always get good traction (even after much pre-event testing with Pirelli), Fiat should have won the event, for there were only two Stratoses (whose luck ran out) and no rivalry at all from Ford. The driver line-up – Röhrl, Andruet, Verini and Darniche – was first class, and the cars (which had been rebuilt after

San Remo 1977) were in tip-top shape. Even so, all of them struggled (and Pirelli was much to blame for this), Röhrl's car broke an electrical connection which cost five special stage minutes, only Röhrl came to terms with the patchy winter weather (and set 11 fastest stage times out of 24), and in the end, the might of Turin was beaten both by the Porsche 911 and, to its shame, two spiritedly-driven front-wheel drive 1.4-litre Renault 5 Alpines! Fourth, fifth, sixth and

Thirty years old? Would you believe it? This was Mick Wood's carefully preserved 131 Abarth, looking just as good as new when captured on a classic event in the UK. (Courtesy Mick Wood)

eighth might have been consistent – but it was consistently not good enough: Röhrl was 3 minutes 19 seconds adrift; without that electrical failure he could have won.

Would Fiat have better luck in Sweden, just a few weeks later? In a way it did, though there was still no victory. Markku Alén notched up third overall, beaten by two factory Ford Escorts that were opening their 1978 programme driven by Björn Waldegård and Hannu Mikkola. As in Monte Carlo, not even the genius of Alén could make up for Ford's definite power advantage. Although Markku

had quite a trouble-free run, he only established three fastest stage times – which compared rather dismally with 16 FTDs (Fastest Time of the Day) for Stig Blomqvist in a Stratos, nine for Hannu Mikkola, and seven for Waldegård. At least Fiat team manager Daniele Audetto had the grace to comment that: "The Ford's have more power, less weight – and success could not go to a nicer person than Ford's Peter Ashcroft."

As in 1977, Fiat then decided not to compete in the Safari which followed over the Easter weekend. Undoubtedly, this was a shrewd move, for not only did Fiat have no experience

If Markku Alén had to name his favourite rallies, Portugal would certainly be one of them. After a stirring, event-long battle with Hannu Mikkola's Ford Escort RS, Markku won the 1978 event outright.

of the African classic (although its housemates at Lancia did), but it readily admitted that the 131 was not engineered to withstand the physical battering which it was likely to get on the unmade roads of Kenya.

Instead, the team stayed home in Turin, remembered just what a boost it had had in winning the Rally of Portugal in 1977, and determined to do it all again. Which it did, but only just, as one lone car (driven by Markku Alén) made it to the finish!

Three 131s started the event, driven by Markku Alén,

Walter Röhrl and (for the very first time) Sandro Munari: Sandro driving a conventional front-engine rear-drive car for the first time in more than a decade. Right from the start, it was clear that this was to be another head-to-head fight, for Ford had entered four Escort RS1800s, and there was also strong competition from Toyota, Vauxhall and Bernard Darniche in an old Lancia Stratos.

Right from the start it was clear that this event, sometimes on tarmac, but often on loose surface stages, was going to be tight for either Fiat or Ford. First Röhrl, then Alén, then

Hurry, hurry, hurry – Markku Alén repeated his previous victory in Portugal by winning outright in 1978. Until the very last stage, he was only seconds ahead of Hannu Mikkola's works Ford Escort.

The 131 Abarths, in good shape, won the Acropolis Rally of 1978, though at one point during the event the driver, Sandro Munari, put his car off the road.

an Escort, and once again a Fiat would lead the event, with only punctures and minor mistakes making a difference, Then came the breakdowns – two of the Fords dropped out (broken half-shafts), Munari's 131 broke wheel studs and found itself stranded, and, at almost the same moment, Röhrl's clutch disintegrated. For the rest of the event, there was battle between Alén's 131 Abarth and Hannu Mikkola's Escort, the difference between them a matter of seconds.

On the last night, only 11 seconds separated the two cars, and before the last stage, there were only four seconds in it. Then, on the last stage, Mikkola's Escort hit a rock, a rear tyre shredded – and Alén was the much-acclaimed victor: Ford's Escorts were second and third, but that was enough. Fiat was euphoric.

It was no wonder that the team went off to tackle the Acropolis Rally, a month later, in very high spirits. Ford,

Fiat 131 Abarths always had to work very hard to finish the ultra-tough Acropolis. This was Walter Röhrl's team car receiving attention in 1978, on its way to outright victory.

pleading poverty, did not compete, so Fiat's three 131 Abarths were only faced with competition from tank-like Datsun 160Js, which could not match the Abarths in performance even though they were known to be very strong.

In Greece, therefore, it was almost a command performance, for Röhrl won the event, defeating team-mate Alén by more than ten minutes, and an analysis of stage times showed that no other make of car was even in the hunt. It was a measure of Fiat's superiority that Röhrl recorded 21 fastest stage times, Alén 12 more, and even Munari (the 131 'novice') made five fastests – and that the nearest rival was Ove Andersson (Toyota Celica), with six FTDs.

Apart from the fact that the 131s suffered some half-shaft trouble (this always seemed to occur on events where Fiat had to provide a lot of wheel travel), they were quite reliable, and the age-old gearbox problems now appeared to be over. Unhappily for Munari, though, his car suffered a broken front differential mounting to the structure.

When the cars appeared in the 1000 Lakes in August, it was almost a 'given' that Markku Alén would dominate proceedings if his 131 stuck

Markku Alén won the Finnish 1000 Lakes in 1978, just as he had in 1976. No wonder it was one of his favourite events.

together – which it duly did. Fiat sent two team cars for Alén and Timo Salonen, and also provided two older cars, on loan, to Autonovo (Finnish Fiat importer) for Simo Lampinen and Hannu Valtaharju.

Although Ford had high hopes of repeating its 1977 success, this was an occasion where the Fiat's high-speed stability and handling paid off once again: the Escorts were not reliable enough to challenge for victory. On this high-speed 'Finnish Grand Prix' (which he had already won, in a 131 Abarth, in 1976) Markku was quite peerless, setting fastest times on 21 of the 45 special stages, and quite comfortably outpacing his team-mate, Timo Salonen, even before Timo rolled his car briefly (he seemed to lose only seconds, rather than minutes!).

Buoyed up by this great success (and by now well ahead of Ford in the Manufacturers' Championship stakes) Fiat then sent a full team of three cars over to Canada, to compete in Quebec. Having won the event in 1977, and found the long, fast stages to its liking, it had very high hopes – particularly as Ford chose not to compete. It need not have worried, it had very little opposition, and no other cars were even on the same pace. Röhrl, Alén and Salonen (Fiat's loose-surface 'A-Team') therefore had a good opportunity to play among themselves. The story of the rally is simply told – Alén led for the first seven stages and Röhrl then led to the finish. One or other of them was fastest on all but one stage, Alén slipped gracefully behind Röhrl from the eighth stage (Team orders? Perish the thought …), watched closely for a time, then slipped gracefully back to be eight minutes off the pace by the close. For Salonen, however, it was not quite as peaceful, as his 131 suffered a multitude of punctures, and the rear axle eventually failed in the middle of a long stage. Undaunted, Fiat used a 'supervision' chase car (a Canadian Plymouth) to push him, bumper to bumper, out of the stage, costing him a $2000 fine but not disqualification.

Although the World Championship battle was theoretically not yet over, a bitter pay strike at Ford then caused Fiat's rivals to miss the next two events. In San Remo, therefore, Fiat's main competition came from Markku Alén's works Lancia Stratos, and from several privately-entered

Porsche 911s. Alén's job was to win the rally, and also to win the FIA Cup for Drivers (a forerunner to the World Drivers' Championship, which would officially begin in 1979), while Fiat's job was to secure the Makes series – though no-one had told it not to compete against Lancia. The result was a domestic scrap, close to home, which left the spectators tingling with excitement.

Although the Alén/Stratos combination (it was Markku's first rally in one of these mid-engined cars) was finally victorious, until the 131 challenge wilted it was always a close battle, especially as San Remo specialist, Sandro Munari, was in the leading 131! Fiat had sent along three reliable 'old nails' – for Munari, Röhrl and Verini – having the very latest in tarmac suspension, engine settings and Pirelli tyres.

Amazingly, the Stratos could not take the lead until Stage 38, as both Munari (14 FTDs) and Walter Röhrl (nine FTDs) set a sparkling pace. Then, unusually, Munari crashed his car on SS18 (reluctantly carrying on the tradition of not finishing any rallies of any type so far in 1978!), while Röhrl crashed on a later special stage which he had practiced thoroughly – and blamed no-one but himself. All of which left Maurizio Verini to finish second to the Stratos, more than ten minutes off the frenetic pace. The likeable Italian upheld Fiat's honour in Italy and put the Championship almost out of reach, he could set only four fastest stage times in the process, but he was always there and thereabouts, behind his illustrious team-mates.

Although Fiat then said that it was not interested in the Bandama Rally (held in the Ivory Coast), it supplied a single rough-road specification car (TOR 88536) for the veteran French star, Jean Vinatier, to drive (currently he was managing the Fiat France team), but did not support it with mechanics. Not that this would have done much good, for the hapless Vinatier hit a truck on a non-competitive section, and the car was too badly damaged to continue.

Then came the Tour de Corse – not exactly home ground for the Fiats, but close enough. Still needing to clinch the Makes title (though the strike-bound Ford team could not turn up), Fiat sent along a full team of identically-specified

84

Here is a rare picture – the works 131 Abarth competing in the Bandama (Ivory Coast) Rally of 1978. French star Jean Vinatier was at the wheel – he eventually retired.

131s – two of them 'official' cars in Alitalia colours for Bernard Darniche and Sandro Munari, and two others in Fiat France livery, to be driven by Jean-Claude Andruet and Michèle Mouton. As usual on this event, the cars were in full tarmac-specification livery, with ultra-wide wheelarch flares, and state-of-the-art Pirelli tyres.

Faced only by two Stratos cars (for Vudafieri and Bettega), and a motley collection of Triumph TR7 V8s and Opels, Fiat should have prepared for another high-speed demonstration, which indeed it did. Unfortunately, Andruet's 131, which led convincingly for much of the time, needed a gearbox change, and this was mis-handled (botched, even) to such an extent that he lost six minutes worth of road penalties to team-mate Bernard Darniche, and lost the rally

The glamour of rallying in a Mediterranean country – a line-up of cars before the start of the 1978 Tour de Corse. No.1 was driven by Bernard Darniche, who won outright.

Michèle Mouton produced several excellent results for Fiat in her Fiat France cars during the 1970s. This car took fifth place in the 1978 Tour de Corse in November 1978 – with three other 131s achieving first, second and third places.

Tight corners, unforgiving crash barriers – but the works cars were at least on home ground. Sandro Munari was rarely successful in 131 Abarths – but here he took fifth place in San Remo in 1978.

by more than four minutes. Conspiracy theorists suggested that Fiat wanted Darniche's official car to win, and not a Fiat France car, though no spokesman ever confirmed this. With wide-eyed innocence, it was suggested that this had merely been unfortunate – but was it just 'unfortunate' that the

work at the service point started late, and took a long time to complete? Amid all this confusion, the good news was that Munari finally finished a rally – in third place – which ended a disheartening sequence for the ex-Lancia star. With a 1-2-3-5 finish, Fiat had much to celebrate.

Yes, co-driver Christian Geistdörfer really is sitting in the centre of the back seat in Walter Röhrl's car in the 1978 RAC Rally. It was a one-off, unsuccessful experiment – and was swiftly banned by the authorities.

With the World Championship for Makes now confirmed, Fiat could afford to relax – so it decided to send only a single 131 Abarth, for Walter Röhrl, to take part in the end-of-season RAC Rally of Great Britain: on the other hand, it also turned up with two Lancia Stratos types, one for Markku Alén (who had fallen in love with this ageing beast), and one for Sandro Munari. Even though Fiat had campaigned one car throughout the 1978 British Rally Championship season – this is detailed overleaf – the fact that it had not recorded a single victory may have been evidence enough that the British 'rough-road' Escort RS was invincible.

But what a car it was! When Walter Röhrl turned up at pre-event scrutineering in Birmingham, it was seen that co-driver Christian Geistdörfer's seat had been placed in the back of the car, in the same area that the normal road car's rear seat would occupy: since pace notes were still banned from this event, there was really not likely to be any communication problem. Was this really going to work? "It's to improve the traction," Geistdörfer explained, "we have tried it in testing, and it improves times by up to a second a mile ..." According to Fiat, much of the testing had been carried out by Georgio Pianta, who had tried out two different positions, one with the co-driver's seat moved simply backwards on his side of the car, the other in the centre of the rear seat area. It was found that the offset position affected the handling badly, so the symmetrically-positioned seat was chosen instead.

No matter. Even though the strike-hit Ford team was running a makeshift 'Dealer Team Ford' operation, the cars, which had been prepared all around the country except at Boreham, were demonstrably faster than the Italian machinery. Both Stratos types eventually retired – one with engine, the other with transmission problems – and though Röhrl was immaculately fast, as ever, he could not keep up with the flying Escorts. Of 76 stages, Röhrl was fastest only three times, while Escorts of various types mopped up 61 FTDs. For Fiat, the result was a disappointing sixth place, and a ruling by officials that the rear co-driver seating position would never again be allowed in a rally car.

Despite this, Fiat had clinched a remarkably successful season for, as Martin Holmes later summarised in an end-of-term report: "Fiat has made the pace at the top end of the sport, it has been the anchor to the sport, it has been the team which has taken the work of development the most seriously – and, as if these contributions have been insufficient, it has created the best on-event entertainment ... Work on the Fiat cars was centred mainly on the engines, units which are the least powerful of any of the leading manufacturers, but which are amazingly easy to use, and coupled with a gearbox which saves seconds against other units on special

stages ... What will happen to World Rallying if and when Fiat ever put a powerful engine into the 131 Abarth begs imagination ..."

Although few fully-tuned 131 Abarths were available to the average private owner (Fiat made sure that its ex-works cars were sold on to deserving teams such as the Jolly Club, and contenders for European Championship events) the cars were well-represented at that level. Although European tarmac events tended to be won by the Lancia Stratos, and gravel events by Ford Escort RS types, 131 became more and more prominent, particularly in Italy, and also in France. Zanini's car won in Poland, while Michèle Mouton won the highly prestigious Tour de France.

This was also the season in which Fiat sent a 131 Abarth to compete in the British Open Rally Championship, originally for Markku Alén to drive, though the policy changed in mid-season. Ultimately, there were no victories, proving that there was no substitute for experience in British forests, for the Fiat was regularly outpaced by one or other of the factory-supported Escorts, notably by Hannu Mikkola. The same car was used throughout the season, going back to Turin for rebuilds. In it, Alén recorded two third places (Circuit of Ireland and the Welsh) while Walter Röhrl took fourth on the Burmah, and Verini, fifth, on the all-tarmac Manx International.

1979

What a difference a year makes. Amazing, isn't it, that a car that had been so dominant in 1978 could seem to struggle so much in 1979? Nothing, it seemed, was ever likely to stop the 131 Abarths from winning whenever and wherever they appeared in 1978 – but a year later, their only success was in the 1000 Lakes, where Markku Alén was on his usual scintillating form.

It wasn't so much that the 131s had slipped backwards, more that the works Escorts had come on so much. Strikes or no strikes, in 1978 the Escorts had had to scratch around to win two rallies (one of them by a quasi-private car), but in 1979 they would win five times, and totally dominate the World Championship. As far as Fiat was concerned, it didn't help that for a time the Italians put a lot of effort into trying to make the front-wheel drive Ritmos into a competitive rally car ...

At the start of the season (need I say 'as usual'?) Fiat struggled to win the ice-bound Monte Carlo and Swedish Rallies, and managed neither. Four works-blessed 131

Abarths started the Monte – those of Alén and Röhrl in Alitalia colours, with Andruet and Michèle Mouton in Fiat France machines which ran to virtually the same specification. Running with slightly detuned engines (Fiat said this was to make them more driveable on ice and snow), they seemed to be slower than in 1978: Ford, on the other hand, had

Oh dear! The miracle is that Walter Röhrl's car actually finished the 1979 Safari Rally in this condition, the result of a collision with a minibus on an open road section.

Three 131 Abarths started the 1979 Safari and three finished – a magnificent achievement. Markku Alén took third place after a storming drive.

produced razor-edge-tuned Escorts that were significantly faster than before. Then there was the Lancia Stratos – or rather, Darniche's old but legendarily successful Stratos – which had everyone else gasping wherever it could get grip. And this was at the kernel of the event. Until the last night, much of the stage mileage was on relatively clear roads, which meant that the 131s were simply outpaced. In the

event, Röhrl's engine broke on the last stage, and the other cars recorded third, fourth and seventh overall, with only a handful of fastest stage times between them. Alén's 131 was more than four minutes off the pace, his drive not helped by illness towards the end.

The sensation of the event, of course, had nothing to do with Fiat. Waldegård's Escort would have won if its progress had not been sabotaged by a rock placed handily in the road, allowing the old Stratos to win instead.

For Fiat it was a similar story in Sweden, though on this occasion there was only a single works 131 to be beaten by its rivals. Theoretically, this was a private entry – for the car carried Marlboro sponsorship, and was quite an old machine – though the usual mechanics were present to keep it going. Markku Alén, as ever, gave it his all, but the car was simply not good enough to keep up with the Fords and (on this very special occasion) with Stig Blomqvist's front-wheel drive Saab 99 Turbo. Competitive? Alén recorded two stage fastests, compared with 19 fastests for Waldegård's Escort, and nine for Blomqvist's Saab.

Amazingly, Fiat then supported two cars to compete in the non-Championship Hankkiralli in the north of Finland, rather than commit machinery to Portugal where it had won so dramatically in 1978. In terms of local publicity, this paid off, for Alén won the event from his temporary team-mate, Ulf Gronholm. On the other hand, not a single 131 Abarth turned up in Portugal – an event which Fiat had previously won in 1977 and 1978 – for the works team had decided to concentrate on getting cars to the East African Safari instead.

As most teams discovered (and Fiat-Lancia, let us not forget, had been to Africa several times in the past with the Lancia Stratos, and so nearly won the event), it was never going to be easy to engineer cars for this hard, rough, dusty and hot event – not to mention wet too, if the rains came early! All in all, it was typical of Fiat's resolve that it not only built three brand new 'heavyweight' cars for this event, but that in the end all those cars (along with private entries for Mike Kirkland and George Githu) also made it to the finish.

When Markku Alén's 131 Abarth won the Finnish 1000 Lakes Rally in 1979, that made it three victories in four years. The 131 Abarth was ideal for Finland's ultra-fast stages.

Although the 131 Abarths did not win – no-one really expected them to – they put on a great operation, in reliability if not in outright performance, though bent and broken rear shock absorbers were a recurrent problem. Alén, Röhrl and Munari all had previous experience on the Safari, albeit in different makes of cars, and all therefore knew how to nurse a car to the finish on this extremely long event. Outpaced by Shekhar Mehta's Datsun 160J, and by Hannu Mikkola in one of the elephantine Mercedes-Benz 450SLC 5.0s, Alén nevertheless managed to finish third overall, though he was no less than 53 minutes off the winning pace.

Walter Röhrl, no doubt, would have finished higher than eighth if he had not first hit a non-competing minibus, and then suffered a smashed windscreen after colliding with a large bird. Much of the side of the car (the driver's side, as it happened) was destroyed, and for hours he had to drive with no screen in place. Several team cars were then held up significantly after one flash flood developed into a complete blockage – but to their relief, this entire section was then cancelled, as most of the field had been unable to proceed, or to find an alternative passage. Later, Röhrl's car broke its steering, Munari's a drive shaft, and all were exhausted. This, though, was absolutely typical of the lottery which was the Safari, an event which still had no special stages, and was held on roads which were all open to the public!

Little wonder, therefore, that no works Fiats turned out on the Acropolis Rally (Fiat-Lancia had hoped that Darniche's Stratos might win, but in the end it broke down and Ford's Björn Waldegård succeeded instead), or that there was no budget available to send cars all the way around the world to compete in New Zealand. However, the team did send two cars to tackle the non-Championship Rally of Brazil, which was due to promote a World Rally in future years, a trip that was certainly worthwhile for it was won by Alén's 131 Abarth, with Röhrl's sister-car behind it, in second place. Otherwise, in a most un-Latin manner, the team stayed at home, re-prepared several cars, and looked forward to the autumn in Europe.

Suddenly, quite suddenly, it seemed, the tide turned, for although just one Alitalia car was sent to Finland for the 1000 Lakes, the ferociously competitive Markku Alén drove it to victory – his third win in four outings, in 131s, in Finland. Not that Fiat was making a big deal of the entry, as (according to the registration number, at least) the car had already completed three earlier World Rallies before it rolled down the ramp in Finland. The Fiat importer, Autonovo, backed up Alén by entering two relatively old works-prepared 131s of its own, one of them driven by a promising newcomer called Henri Toivonen.

This was a close, hard-fought battle, which either Alén or Ari Vatanen (in a works Ford Escort) might have won, and Hannu Mikkola's Escort led both of them until his engine head gasket let go. If Vatanen had not gone off

the road, briefly, on one stage towards the end of the event, who knows who might have won – but in the end it was Alén, with 22 fastest stage times (against Vatanen's 20), who won the rally by a mere 91 seconds. Although World Championship success was now out of the question, at least the team's morale had been restored.

Not that it stayed high for long. Fiat did not send cars to Quebec (where Ford's Escorts finished first and third), and on San Remo, two out of the three works 131s suffered severe transmission problems. Ford didn't enter, but there was an old Jolly Club-entered Lancia Stratos which made all the running and which did, in the end, win the event.

The three works 131s were the latest 'quick-change' specification – tarmac or gravel suspension could be used, for there were both types of stage on this event – but there was no more power than before, as the 16-valve engine was resolutely limited to 230bhp, a deficiency which irritated the drivers. Alén, Röhrl and Attilio Bettega drove the cars, but it was only Röhrl's and Alén's unearthly driving skills on well-practised stages which kept them up close to the Stratos. Fiat, no doubt, would have liked to apply team orders (and they do say that 'certain approaches' were made to the Jolly Club, who relied on Fiat-Lancia's patronage in so many ways), but this did not seem to happen. Alén fell out of contention with a broken gearbox, then a broken differential – repairs cost him no less than 16 minutes on the road – but Röhrl (second) and Bettega (third) did remarkably well, and made it to the finish.

For Fiat, then, the season was almost over – and none too successful it had been – so the team ignored Corsica which followed (it left Fiat France to hold up the flag, for whom Michèle Mouton took fifth place), and it was only stubbornness, and the ambition of Walter Röhrl, which saw a single car entered for Britain's RAC Rally at the end of the season. Markku Alén persuaded the company to prepare a Stratos for this event, and, in fact, he led for the first ten stages, before being annihilated by the fleet of works Escorts. In the single 131 Abarth driven by Röhrl, there was no sign of the rear-seat co-driver's position which had been a feature of the 1978 event. Number-plate watchers spotted that this car

Walter Röhrl was always the most polished and clinically accurate of Fiat's works drivers. Here he was on his way to second place in the 1979 San Remo Rally.

had been seen throughout the 1978 British Championship series (never quite managing to win an event), but it had of course been completely refurbished. Although Röhrl was his usual immaculate self, his car simply could not keep up with the fleet of Ford Escorts (which finished first, second, fourth and sixth), and it is significant that he set only two fastest stage times, both of them recorded in mid-Wales, on the final night, when the pressure was off.

This, then, was the end of what had been rather a disappointing season for Fiat. So dominant in 1978, it

seemed to have been out-paced in 1979 – and it was only the promise of a 'Ford-free' season in 1980 (for Boreham was temporarily closing its doors to develop a new car) which buoyed its spirits.

At European level, however, 131 Abarths were now winning with some regularity, recording no fewer than twelve outright victories and a host of minor placings. On events like this, where tarmac was more often seen than gravel, the 131 Abarth was ideal. In the UK, however, another assault on the British Championship failed completely. Timo Salonen

95

Walter Röhrl never won the British RAC Rally because he did not enjoy 'blind' stages without pace notes. He finished eighth on this event in 1979.

rolled the car down a bank on the Circuit of Ireland, and it had to be repaired comprehensively in England immediately afterwards. Markku Alén started the Welsh Rally, but retired on the first stage with a broken drive shaft, while Timo Salonen could not get among the leaders in the Scottish before a failed fuel injection pump immobilised the engine, just two stages from home. The team would have been more suited to the Manx and Ulster events (where all the stages were tarmac, and where pace notes were allowed) but it did not appear, and the season was therefore over.

No-one was hurt, thank goodness, but this was not a moment which Fiat cherished. Timo Salonen had been pushing hard on the 1979 Circuit of Ireland, but went over the edge on this special stage.

This was the newly-liveried works 131 Abarth, as revealed before the start of the 1980 season. Alitalia sponsorship had been phased out in favour of this corporate scheme.

1980

Fiat now took a deep breath, planned ahead for 1980, and was coldly determined to take back the Makes Championship from Ford, who had won it rather comfortably in 1979. There was a touch of typically-Latin doublespeak in the early pre-season announcements when Fiat insisted that it would not enter events just because it might gain some points, that some events were commercially more important than others, and so on, and so on. It was not until July, with Fiat and Walter Röhrl leading the Makes and Drivers'

Championships convincingly, that the official change of heart came about.

This time around there would be few competitive Fords (though the new David Sutton-Rothmans team, using works drivers, was a potential threat), and surely it would only be Latin incompetence which would cause problems? The fact that the team had lost its Alitalia sponsorship, and was now running in a corporate colour scheme, was not considered critical. Neither was the fact that Sandro Munari was no longer driving for the team, as in 1980 there was a surplus of good drivers (such as Björn Waldegård) available on the freelance market. The record shows, in fact, that the only new competition came from Talbot, who embarked on a serious World programme with its Sunbeam-Lotus: this was a car often described as 'a better Escort,' but the team was hampered by a limited budget. As in 1979, the major competition really came from Datsun, whose cars were strong enough, if not fast enough, to trouble Fiat on sealed surfaces.

Although Fiat built very few brand new cars in 1980 (the record shows that we only saw six new identities throughout the season), they were impressively reliable. There were few unplanned breakdowns and, as the results summary confirmed, works 131 Abarths started almost every World event, notched up five outright victories, and stood on the podium (in second and third places) on five other occasions.

Technically, of course, the 131 Abarth had long since reached maturity, and even by this time the parent company had begun to start thinking about its successor, which would be a Lancia (the Rally 037). On every event, therefore, it meant that the

team could concentrate on building 'standard' cars, draw heavily on experience from the previous years, and rely on the superstar drivers to add the extra bit of 'stardust' to the performance. Pirelli's contribution should again be stressed, for the giant Italian tyre supplier certainly spent a great deal of time in joint development with Fiat, which was, after all, one of its most important commercial customers!

The magic appeared immediately. On a Monte Carlo Rally which was, in places, devoid of the expected snow and ice, Walter Röhrl gained the victory which Fiat thought it had deserved for years. With less ice (and with a younger car), Bernard Darniche and his ancient Lancia Stratos might have won the event (he finished second, though ten minutes adrift), for he set ten fastest stage times. Although Fiat

Walter Röhrl pressing on over hard-packed snow and ice at the top of the Col du Turini, on his way to victory in the 1980 Monte Carlo Rally.

Mouton finished a solid seventh in the other Fiat France machine. All in all, everyone seemed to be happy, and Fiat's World programme had started as Cesare Fiorio meant it to go on.

Which it duly did in Sweden. Even though only one competitive 131 Abarth was entered, it was driven by Björn Waldegård (the same car with which he had finished third in Monte Carlo), who was his usual unspectacular self. If there was an omen on this event, it was that Anders Kulläng's Opel Ascona 400 won outright, a maiden win for the big car which was to become more and more competitive as the next two seasons progressed. Fast, but not quite fast enough, Björn was rewarded by another third place.

Then came Portugal, an event which the 131 Abarth had already won in 1977 and 1978, though in order to concentrate on the Safari, the team had not even turned up in 1979. This time, though, the 'A-Team' – Alén, Röhrl and Bettega – turned up in cars running to a very familiar specification, and before the start there was an assurance that there were no team orders, though Röhrl always appeared to be the 'favourite' son.

Because the 131 Abarth soon proved to be quite dominant on this event (and with so much previous experience in Portugal, it should have been ...) there was no need to favour any of the drivers, for only Bernard Darniche (in his old Stratos) could offer much resistance, leading the rally until the engine dropped a valve. As it happened, the works 131s set 32 fastest stage times out of 47 stages, 18 of them by Walter Röhrl and 14 by Alén. Bettega could not

insisted that it was concentrating on the development of the new Ritmo front-wheel drive car (a 1.5-litre machine), it still produced five cars for Monte Carlo – two official cars, two for Fiat France, and one for Fiat Sweden (World Champion Björn Waldegård drove that car).

Things did not necessarily go according to plan. Markku Alén's car got no further than the second stage, where it slid off the road, hit a tree and damaged the front suspension. From this moment on, Walter Röhrl took the lead in the sister car and never lost it, though there was a scare at one point when the ignition pack on his car failed on a road section, and more than twenty minutes were lost before it could be replaced. Of the others, Waldegård took time to get used to a new car, but eventually took third place, Jean-Claude Andruet put his Fiat France car off the road, yet Michèle

Spectator control in some Mediterranean countries – this was Portugal in 1980 – was frighteningly casual. This was Markku Alén, on his way to second place. Team-mate Walter Röhrl won the event.

(Opposite) Walter Röhrl pressing on in the dreadfully dusty conditions of Greece, 1980. The result – fifth place.

(Above) No time to stand and stare. This was picturesque scenery taken at high speed in 1980.

match them, and suffered a road accident before the end of the very first day. This was an event where Röhrl had all the luck and Alén all the disasters, for his car suffered from a failed electrical alternator, and needed not one but three differential changes. Röhrl won the event by a total of 14 minutes, and took a lead in the World Drivers' Championship which he was never to lose.

With no entry in the Safari, Fiat could concentrate on sending the full works team to compete in the Acropolis Rally in Greece, at the end of May. Having won the event in 1978, Fiat thought it should do so again, especially as there were no works Escorts to get in the way. Unhappily for them, though, Ari Vatanen was on top form, his latest Rothmans Escort seemed to be as good as any Boreham car had ever been, and the outcome was that Markku Alén could only take third place (second went to Timo Salonen in a sturdy Datsun 160J).

Fiat didn't even find it all that easy. First of all, Alén was held up in dust clouds as he caught up with other competitors, Röhrl complained about his car's handling, and Bettega was simply not quite fast enough. Alén then suffered yet another transmission failure (propeller shaft rather than gearbox) and lost no less than 17 minutes on the road, and Bettega's car was plagued by – guess what? – problems with the gearbox. Even then it wasn't over, for Bettega's car then holed its sump after a series of hard landings on rough stages, while Walter Röhrl apparently misheard a pace note, went off the road, and needed a squadron of spectators to push him back on a gain: fortune finally smiled on Fiat, however, as that stage was subsequently cancelled because of other irregularities!

The stats, tell their own story. On a 55 stage event, Vatanen's Escort was fastest 27 times, while the best the Fiats could do was seven for Röhrl, and two for Alén. Even so, third and fifth (Alén and Röhrl) was some reward for an exhausting weekend, and World Championship positions were reinforced.

Fiat then gathered together all its budget, consulted Alitalia on ways of getting cars to South America, and travelled out to Argentina in July to tackle the next World event with no fewer than five rally cars and a squad of practice cars, too. Not only did it provide cars for all the usual drivers – Röhrl, Alén and Bettega – and hired a car for Francisco Mayorga too, but it also provided a mount for Argentina F1 hero Carlos Reutemann. Those at Fiat were no fools – for not only was the signing of Reutemann a major coup, but he also brought with him a mass of local sponsorship (reputed to be US$300,000) which defrayed expenses considerably.

Since the only real competition came from Datsun (with two 8-valve 160Js) and from Mercedes-Benz (with three 500SLCs and a 280E), Fiat was firmly expected to win in its Safari-specification cars. This it duly did, for Walter Röhrl led from start to finish, setting fastest times on ten of the 14 special stages, and never looking likely to be beaten.

As usual (for 1980 at least) it was Markku Alén who suffered the ill-luck: not only did he lose 15 minutes at one point, when his car was reputedly re-fuelled with diesel instead of petrol fuel, but both he and Bettega were eventually forced out when heavy landings on a bumpy stage saw them retire with broken sumps, a loss of oil, and subsequent engine failure. Röhrl, need one point out, was lucky in that one of his high jumps bent a chassis side member, but not the engine sump, so he was able to carry on, though with a less-than-perfect 131 Abarth! Even Reutemann was not immune, for he got his car stuck in a ford for at least 20 minutes before help came in the shape of mechanics from a Fiat-hired helicopter. Fortunately for Fiat, Datsun and Mercedes-Benz were also afflicted by problems. Mikkola's 500SLC had a complete brake failure at one point, while Waldegård's sister car suffered from two drive shaft failures, so Fiat held its breath and eventually made it to the finish.

It is a measure of the event's toughness, and the problems suffered by everyone, that Röhrl's winning margin

Dust, altitude and sheer gruelling endurance were all part of the Rally of Argentina in 1980. Walter Röhrl's works car won the event, though this machine, driven by Attilio Bettega, had to drop out with a damaged engine.

All the drama of a special stage on a steep, hairpinned part of the route in Argentina in 1980. Works 131 Abarths would take first and third places overall – one of them driven by F1 driver Carlos Reutemann.

over Mikkola's big Mercedes-Benz was 16 minutes, with Carlos Reutemann a further 31 minutes behind. And yes, those intervals, quoted in minutes, not seconds, were correct!

By this point of the season, Markku Alén needed a boost to his morale. Fortunately this came in the following month, when his 131 Abarth won the 1000 Lakes in his native Finland, and he notched up his fourth victory in five years!

Fiat must indeed have been confident in the potential of the Alén-131 combination, for his was the only such car it supported on the event. The car, in fact, was actually entered by Autonovo (the Finnish Fiat importer), and was a machine which Alén and Björn Waldegård had driven in Scandinavia earlier in the year: it had been re-prepared in Finland, and there was no sign of the normal 1980-type works livery. This re-preparation project was now easily possible because engineering rally development of the 131 Abarth had now virtually concluded, so the 1980 car ran with precisely the same set-up as that which had won the event in 1979. Except in one detail, that is – Pirelli had brought along the very latest tyres which had made the works Fiats so lastingly competitive throughout the year.

Despite the fact that this was an event which Markku Alén was always coldly capable of winning – and had often done so! – the 131 Abarth could easily have been beaten, not least by Ari Vatanen's Rothmans Escort RS, and by sundry Vauxhalls, Opels and even Henri Toivonen's Talbot Sunbeam-Lotus. The statistics show, however, that although

It always helped to have good waterproofing. Walter Röhrl's car thunders through a water-splash in the 1980 Rally of Argentina. He led the event from start to finish.

none of them ever looked like actually beating Alén, who led the event from start to finish, and was fastest on 25 of the 47 stages, and second fastest on 21 more, it was always a close battle. Vatanen, in the Escort RS, was fastest on almost every other stage, and the winning gap was a mere 56 seconds – an average of little more than one second for every stage.

Then came Fiat's entry in its second 'flyaway' event of the year – this time to New Zealand, where the 131 Abarths had won once before in 1977. Held in mid-September, the Motogard event was run at an awkward time of year for Fiat (just two weeks after the 1000 Lakes, and three weeks before San Remo), which probably explains why there had been no mass attendance in Finland in August. Although it pleaded relative poverty before the event (reputedly, it was not only

By Markku Alén's Finnish standards, that is not a very high jump – he was pressing on to yet another well-deserved victory in the 1000 Lakes Rally in 1980.

Style, sheer style from team leader Walter Röhrl's works 131 Abarth, on his way to second place in the Rally of New Zealand in 1980.

running out of funds, but of fresh and competitive cars), Fiat needed to score well to get the World Championship title in its sights.

Once again there was just a single car in the lists. This was actually the ex-Argentina car, driven by Röhrl to victory, which had been flown straight from one continent (in July) to another. Re-preparation was carried out in New Zealand

in the weeks leading up to the start.

The German had clearly been instructed to finish at all costs, no further down than third if it could be arranged, and not to break his car, nor go off the road, in the fruitless pursuit of ultimate glory.

The contest soon settled down to a battle between Röhrl, Timo Salonen (Datsun 160J) and Pentti Airikkala

For San Remo in 1980, a factory strike caused Fiat to borrow other cars for its works drivers. Team leader Walter Röhrl used a lightweight test car which was entered by the Jolly Club, and which did not carry corporate livery – he won the event by more than six minutes.

(ex-works Ford Escort RS), for the big Mercedes-Benz cars were too big and cumbersome for this event. Those three drivers shared almost all the fastest stage times, but, except for a brief point on the second day, it was Timo Salonen who led throughout, gradually pulling out a lead from which he would not be dislodged. Airikkala finally had a big accident, which destroyed his Escort and put him in hospital with a back injury for a period, and Röhrl gradually used up his precious stock of tyres which had also been flown over from Argentina. In the end, he was 2 minutes 41 seconds behind Salonen, but Fiat's and Röhrl's positions, at the top of the relevant Championship tables, had both been strengthened, and with two 'close-to-home' rallies now ahead (San Remo and Corsica), Fiat thought it could relax just a little.

But – suddenly – a crisis erupted. San Remo followed New Zealand by less than three weeks, and in these weeks the works team was suddenly embroiled in a strike which paralysed the factory and made completion of authentic cars for the event quite impossible: not even the motorsport-mad Italian unions could be persuaded to relax their grip, or turn a blind eye.

It was an example of Fiat's power and influence that three supposedly 'private' cars were found at very short notice. Team leader, Walter Röhrl, used a works car still painted in virgin white (which had, quite fortuitously, been working at the Fiat test track remote from the factories), and was entered by the Jolly Club. Markku Alén was introduced to a car normally driven by 'Lucky' for the Quattro Rombi team, and Attilio Bettega used a car from the River Team Racing Équipe. It wasn't an ideal solution, though it was a solution of sorts. As team principal, Cesare Fiorio, commented at the time: "We have plenty of service vans, and plenty of people, but we do not have the spares or the special tools to keep the cars in the rally ..."

The miracle is that, just as Ford's team had triumphed over the strikers in the 1978 RAC Rally, so Fiat triumphed in San Remo, in 1980. The attitude, that nothing so trivial as a company-wide strike was going to stop it, served well, and Walter Röhrl eventually came home first, well over six minutes ahead of Ari Vatanen and Hannu Mikkola's Rothmans

Escort RSs. It was a measure of the tight competition that five different drivers held the lead at one point, and that no fewer than nine different drivers set fastest stage times in this week-long event of 49 stages.

Bettega's rally was ruined in the first hour when his car dropped the prop shaft onto the road (yes, really!), and the likeable Italian spent the rest of the event trying to make up 13 lost minutes, though later he also rolled his borrowed car, and had to ease off. Alén was fast to begin with – he led the rally at the end of the first day – but the engine soon wilted and began to pump lots of oil out of a breather, so he was forced to retire. Röhrl, on the other hand, kept steadily on, setting fastest times wherever possible (he would record 17 fastests before the end of this six-day marathon), and taking over the outright lead after his big rival, Ari Vatanen, crumpled the tail of his Rothmans Escort in an accident.

Walter Röhrl won the San Remo Rally of 1980 using what had previously been an Abarth test car. Although merely a 'lightweight' machine, it survived an event with many gravel stages, and beat all its opposition.

was abandoned, which brought Fiat's season to a close. At the same time, too, Walter Röhrl reported that although he might have become World Rally Champion, he was about to leave and join Mercedes-Benz, while Markku Alén, who had had many disgruntled hours in 1980, tried to decide if he should leave or not – but in the end, he stayed.

Cesare Fiorio insisted that the company had spent all its budget and more in winning this Championship, and that there would not be the same level of funding for 1981, which is perhaps one reason why he did not try too hard to keep Röhrl on the books. There was no 131 Abarth successor in sight, though the Lancia Rally 037 had started testing.

One step down from World events, at European Championship level, the 131 Abarth was still one of the best and most versatile cars to use, and during the season such cars won eight events outright, and were often filling minor placings too. In 1980, though, there was no perseverance in British rallies, where Fiat had concluded that it could not hope to beat a fleet of Escorts in their home forests.

1981

When the four-wheel drive Audi Quattro was homologated on 1 January 1981, the world of rallying changed forever. Although Fiat was not yet convinced that the Quattro could swamp the 131 Abarth completely, it was clear that there was now no untapped potential in its own car. Worse – for 1981 it had lost the services of World Champion, Walter Röhrl, who had defected to Mercedes-Benz (which promptly aborted its programme, thus putting him out of work!).

For 1981, therefore, Fiat-Lancia's works team concentrated on the secret design and development of a car which would become the new Lancia Rally 037, while completing a low-key rally programme with the existing 131 Abarth. A look at the identity of cars used suggests that the team was effectively using up the existing fleet of old vehicles – or at least, old registration numbers: only one new car – Markku Alén's Portugal car – was used during a season in which the team scored on just five events, and took just a single victory.

Starting the season quietly, Fiat entered just two works

Although his car was never ideal for this rally – it had been built only in tarmac specification, and could not be adjusted to loose-surface conditions – the pragmatic Röhrl gritted his teeth, kept going, and finally won. The gallant Bettega eventually scrambled into sixth place, 25 minutes behind Röhrl – and Fiat's position as winner of the 1980 World Championship for Makes was assured.

Only two weeks later, the World Rallying 'circus' moved from mainland Italy to the island of Corsica. Somehow, in that time, Italy's trades unions had been made to see sense and the cars which might have competed in San Remo were released so that they could compete in Corsica. However, this big rush meant that although the cars were mechanically perfect, they were not properly painted up in the corporate colours. Walter Röhrl, Attilio Bettega and Bernard Darniche drove (Markku Alén was already preparing to drive a Lancia Stratos in the Giro d'Italia), and with two cars from Fiat France (Jean-Claude Andruet and Michèle Mouton), this was a formidable entry.

Was it asking too much for most of these cars to win? Indeed it was – for the stats show that Darniche and Bettega both crashed on Corsica's narrow and serpentine roads (Darniche after clashing with Frequelin's works Talbot Sunbeam-Lotus), while Andruet's engine broke with a deranged camshaft timing belt. Engine failure was a 131 Abarth affliction which was never really cured in six years of serious rallying. Nor did the 131 Abarth seem to be ideal for this particular event, as only Andruet seemed to be competitive (before his engine blew ...), and Michèle Mouton's died for a time after being swamped by slushy water, which dropped her from second to fifth.

In, around, and somehow apart from all this, Röhrl drove at what, for him, seemed to be less than full pace, happy to take second place to Thérier's Porsche 911, and therefore confirming his Drivers' Championship crown.

Within hours, it seemed, Fiat decided not to take up starting places in the RAC Rally. Original plans had been to send a full team, and then this had been scaled down to just a single entry for Bettega ("... just for fun, he hasn't done the RAC Rally before," said a spokesman), but finally even that

When Markku Alén won in Portugal in 1981, it was that model's fourth Portuguese victory in five years.

cars in the Monte, for team-leader Markku Alén and Dario Cerrato to drive: both cars had already been seen in 1980. With most of the media attention concentrating on the new Audi Quattros (both of which retired!), it was a miracle that anyone noticed them, especially as the 131 Abarth was way off the pace on this ice-and-snow event. In the end, Alén took seventh place, totally disillusioned with his lack of grip, and without a single competitive time to console him.

Predictably, therefore, Fiat then ignored the snow-bound Swedish Rally, but put in a massive three-car

effort in Portugal (an event which the 131 had previously won in 1977, 1978 and 1980). In a week when the very first of the Lancia Rally 037 'mules' was caught testing by a spy camera, Fiat enjoyed its victory in Portugal as a useful diversion. Not only did Markku Alén's car survive a major accident, but it set nine fastest stage times and won outright.

Although Markku spun off wildly on the fourth stage – he needed to drag the car off the stage with a front wheel completely missing – the mechanics then did a speedy and major rebuilding job, after which the Finn began the long

By 1981 the 131 Abarth was close to retirement, but it needed another geriatric old rally car – Ari Vatanen's Escort RS – to beat Markku Alén's car in the 1000 Lakes Rally. He finished second overall and was always on the pace.

struggle to get back on terms. Because Hannu Mikkola's Quattro led for half the rally, Alén's team-mates both crashed their 131s when trying to keep up, but a grim-faced Markku kept it going, and finally took the lead soon after the Quattro's engine let go, and Vatanen's Escort crashed.

In the end, the 131 won the event by a massive 9 minutes 10 seconds which was not actually a measure of its superiority, but of the way almost all the opposition had fallen. Although we did not know it, this was the last World

victory a 131 would ever have.

Once again, after this Fiat stepped back and ignored the Safari and Corsica, but then entered two new-old cars (both of them carried 1979 identities but had new body shells!) for Alén and Bettega to drive on the Acropolis. As every rally enthusiast surely knows, this was an event won by Ari Vatanen in his Rothmans Escort, in which the works Quattros were thrown out for technical infringements – but the two 131s kept going to finish strongly in second and third places. Although they set only four fastest stages times (out of 55) between them, both cars were consistently fast, and withstood the heat, dust and rocks of Greece with remarkable reliability. Although they never led the event they were never out-paced, and once the Quattros had been disqualified, the contest was once again wide open. Fiat had mountains of experience by this stage, and knew that just one piece of over-exuberance by Vatanen would have delivered another famous victory.

It was three months before works 131s once again appeared at World level – on the Finnish 1000 Lakes where just one car (another new-old example) was entered for Markku Alén to drive. Because Markku had won four out of the previous five 1000 Lakes events in 131 Abarths he had

high hopes, but suffered a high-speed roll (which amazingly cost him only seconds), and intermittent electrical faults, which were probably connected with that accident. Stage for stage, it seemed, Markku had been as fast as Vatanen and his Rothmans Escort RS, and eventually lost out by just 59 seconds. Although he was not best pleased, he was probably lucky to finish so high up, as Mikkola's Quattro was dominating the event until an engine camshaft change was required, and dropped him back to third place.

In a final fling in front of the home crowd, Fiat then entered no fewer than four works cars in the San Remo Rally – for Alén, Bettega, Cerrato and Vudafieri – all of which were well-used machines. Cerrato's car was (nominally, at least) so old that it carried a 1977 identity, while two more were

The works 131 Abarth's very last outing was in the 1981 San Remo, where Markku Alén took a modest ninth place.

1978-build models!

In a rally dominated by four-wheel drive Audi Quattros, the suddenly-aged Fiat looked, and was, off the pace, whether on tarmac or on gravel. Although Alén and Cerrato both recorded three fastest stage times each, that was no more than a flourish. In the end two of the cars were eliminated in accidents, Alén dropped out of contention when his gearbox needed to be replaced, which left Cerrato eighth and the unhappy Finn ninth: he, at least, could look forward to better things, with the new Lancia in 1982 …

At European level, ex-works 131 Abarths appeared in many events, recording eight outright victories and many

A bird's eye view of Parc Ferme, in the middle of the 1981 San Remo Rally at Siena. Two works 131 Abarths, carrying the blue Fiat corporate livery, finished the rally. One is third from the left in the top row, one on the extreme left in the bottom row.

minor placings. Additionally, the young Italian, Adartico Vudafieri, used a 131 Abarth to win the European Rally Championship by a country mile.

1982

Quite suddenly thereafter, the 131 Abarth disappeared from top-class rallying. Having previewed the new Lancia Rally 037 at the end of 1981, the factory now concentrated on its development and homologation, giving the new mid-engined machine its World debut in Corsica in May. Now regularly beaten by the latest Opel Ascona 400s – apart from two European Championship victories by Andrea Zanussi, in Spain and in Bulgaria – the 131 Abarth virtually disappeared from the scene, and its top-line career came speedily to a close.

Replacing the 131 Abarth – the Group B dilemma

By 1979, Fiat realised that the 131 Abarth had reached the zenith of its capabilities, and that if the marque was to stay in motorsport in the 1980s, a replacement model was required. Unhappily, however, this was a moment at which the parent company was agonising over the marketing stance of its two major brands – Fiat and Lancia. By performing not one, but two somersaults, the company reversed the decision made only in 1975.

That was the time, of course, when Fiat and Lancia had both been in rallying, and were effectively competing against each other. Lancia's Stratos was dominant, with the Fiat 124 Abarth Rallye struggling to become competitive. The 131 Abarth had then been developed to take over from the 124 Abarth Rallye – and from 1977 it was decided to put the rally emphasis on the mass-market Fiat, at the expense of Lancia. From then until the early 1980s, the 131 Abarth would become the company's rally car weapon, while Lancia would develop more and yet more fierce evolutions of the Beta Monte Carlo for circuit racing.

Then, in 1980, came the second marketing somersault, and the decision was heavily influenced by the FIA's decision to introduce a new set of sporting categories – Groups N,

A and B – to replace the old Groups 1, 2, and 4. In the same way as late 1970s rallying had been all about building the best Group 4 machines, from 1982 the game would inevitably shift, to building Group B cars.

Once Fiat had spent time trying (but failing) to make a competitive rally car out of the front-wheel drive Ritmo, there was no other obvious modern Fiat which could be used as the basis of a new Group B car. This, allied to the growing conviction that Lancia rather than Fiat should uphold the Group's honour in motorsport, meant that the 131 Abarth and the Ritmo projects were allowed to die gracefully, and that future projects would use a Lancia badge. Since that time, no Fiat-badged car has ever shown in World Rallying.

From 1980, therefore, a successor to the Group 4 131 Abarth took shape, but it would be known as the Lancia Rally 037 – the '037' being the project number of the new model – and would be a Group B car, of which only 200

It needed a very special car to improve on the 131 Abarth, and the Lancia Rally 037 was. This type of supercharged, mid-engined Group B model, for which Sergio Limone led the Abarth engineering team, was used between 1981 and 1985.

The Lancia Rally 037 took over from the Fiat 131 Abarth in 1982, and featured a supercharged derivative of the 131 Abarth's 2-litre engine.

examples would have to be made. Although the cars carried different badges, and looked entirely different, the technical link between them was strong. Not only were they both engineered within Abarth, remote from the main Fiat-Lancia technical centre, but Ing. Sergio Limone, who had been working on 131 Abarth development since its origin, was to be the chief designer of the new 037.

Apart from the fact that the new Rally 037 used a derivative of the same 16-valve engine as the 131 Abarth, it was totally different from the Fiat. Based very loosely around the steel tub of the two-seater Lancia Monte Carlo, the 037 had a mid-mounted engine behind the cabin, the engine itself was supercharged, and it drove the rear wheels through a five-speed ZF transaxle. In road car trim, the engine produced 210bhp, and in rally car tune it produced 310bhp. Caught by spy cameras early in 1981, the definitive 037 Rally was officially unveiled in December, homologation followed in April 1982, and it started winning, at World level, in 1983.

This was the road car version of the Lancia Rally 037. Fiat-Lancia needed to build 200 cars to secure Group B homologation, and speedily achieved this in 1981-1982.

World/major European rally wins

Works-prepared 131 Abarth types won these events at World level:

Event	Car	Drivers
1976		
1000 Lakes	TON94414	Alén/Kivimaki
1977		
Portugal	TOP35977	Alén/Kivimaki
South Pacific		
(New Zealand)	TOP21499	Bacchelli/Rossetti (Local reg: IG7925)
Quebec	TON92968	Salonen/Markkula
San Remo	TOR19729	Andruet/Delferrier
Tour de Corse	TOR19728	Darniche/Mahé
1978		
Portugal	TOP35975	Alén/Kivimaki
Acropolis	TOR88538	Röhrl/Geistdörfer
1000 Lakes	TOR92451	Alén/Kivimaki
Quebec	TOR88538	Röhrl/Geistdörfer
Tour de Corse	TOR19730	Darniche/Mahé
1979		
1000 Lakes	TOP35975	Alén/Kivimaki
1980		
Monte Carlo	TOT95329	Röhrl/Geistdörfer
Portugal	TOR92448	Röhrl/Geistdörfer
Argentina	TOR92448	Röhrl/Geistdörfer
1000 Lakes	TOP88538	Alén/Kivimaki
San Remo	TOV33681	Röhrl/Geistdörfer

Event	Car	Drivers
1981		
Portugal	TOV39606	Alén/Kivimaki
San Remo	TOV33681	Röhrl/Geistdörfer
1981		
Portugal	TOV39606	Alén/Kivimaki

Works rally cars
(and when first used)

Note: Like all other serious works rally teams of the 1960s, 1970s and 1980s, some registration numbers appeared on more than one car. On occasion, if the monocoque of a 131 was too badly damaged to repair, a new car would be built up and prepared for motorsport, but using the old chassis plate and identity.

According to factory records, a grand total of 50 works cars were prepared in six years. A handful of these were used as test cars, or were not used in major-league rallies. Except in one special case, all are identified here by their Turin-based (TO ....) registration numbers:

1976
TOK95989
TON19169
TON72918
TON72919
TON72920
TON94410
TON92969
TON92970
TON92971
TON92976
TON94414
TON94415
TOP09881

1977
TON92791
TON92792
TON92968
TOP06217
TOP14398
TOP21499

TOP35972
TOP35973
TOP35974
TOP35976
TOP35977
TOP43573
TOP51473
TOP88538
TOP92972
TOR19728
TOR19729
TOR19730
TOR19731
TOR37173

1978
TOP35975
TOR62948
TOR88536
TOR88537
TOR88538
TOR88539

TOR92415
TOR92451

1979
TOR92448
TOR92452
TOR92453
TOR92559
TOT92359

1980
PD514333 (Quattro Rombi team – used on San Remo 1980)
TOR92449
TOR92450
TOT93356
TOU48219
TOV33680
TOV33681

1981
TOV39606

RALLY GIANTS

Stratos
Lancia

Graham Robson

ISBN: 978-1-787111-10-3
- **Paperback • 128 pages**
- **Over 100 colour and mono pictures**

The Audi Quattro was the world's first successful four-wheel-drive rally car. It brought new standards to the sport, and inspired many others to copy it. This is the complete story. Packed with illustrations, technical details, facts, figures and successes of this innovative car, this book is a must for any rally fan.

RALLY GIANTS

Quattro
Audi

Group B
Sport
Sport S1

Graham Robson

ISBN: 978-1-787111-08-0
Paperback • 19.5x21cm • 128 pages
- **131 colour and b&w pictures**

This book describes the birth, development and rallying career of the Lancia Stratos, Europe's very first purpose-built rally car, in the mid/late 1970s, providing a compact and authoritative history of where, when and how it became so important to the sport. Also tells the story of the team.

For more information and price details, visit our website at www.veloce.co.uk • email: info@veloce.co.uk
• Tel: +44(0)1305 260068

eBook ISBN 978-1-845849-53-5

• available as an eBook • 400 mainly colour pictures

Written with affection, appreciation and authority – and criticism where it is due – Porsche's rally story is a subject that any rally fan will find compelling. Written by lifelong Porsche enthusiast and world authority Laurence Meredith, this is a comprehensive study of Porsche's occasional foray into the world of international rallying. Illustrated with 400 photographs and with details of every rally car, it is a must for any Porsche or motorsport fanatic.

helped to bring the mighty Mini to the fore of international rallying and racing. Includes many previously unseen photos of the car's development, copies of Rover's internal documents, and pages from the road books of top rallies.

eBook ISBN 978-1-845847-13-5

• available as an eBook • 500+ illustrations

This unique book highlights how the use of distributor-less ignition, six speed gearboxes and modern tyres all

ISBN: 978-1-845849-94-8
Paperback • 25x20.7cm • 192 pages

• 217 pictures

Reprinted after a long absence! For the London to Sydney Marathon, team instructions included the recommendation that a firearm be carried by the crew of each car ... "A small pistol which can conveniently be located under cover in the car is what we have in mind" ...

eBook ISBN 978-1-845847-23-4

• available as an eBook • 330 pictures

This book covers the pre-WRC golden years, the Rally of the Forest period. With access to crew notes and manufacturers' archives, and containing many previously unpublished pictures, the history and excitement of the RAC International Rally of Great Britain has been captured in *RAC Rally Action!*

For more information and price details, visit our website at www.veloce.co.uk

• email: info@veloce.co.uk • Tel: +44(0)1305 260068

Index

Note: There are so many repeated references to Abarth, Fiat, and 131 Abarth, in the text, that it is impractical to index them.